INGLÊS

ENSINO FUNDAMENTAL

Edgar Laporta

9º ano

1ª EDIÇÃO
SÃO PAULO
2012

Coleção Eu Gosto Mais
Inglês 9º ano
© IBEP, 2012

Diretor superintendente	Jorge Yunes
Gerente editorial	Célia de Assis
Editor	Angelo Gabriel Rozner
Assistente editorial	Fernanda dos Santos Silva
Revisão técnica	Mariett Regina R. de Azevedo
Revisão	Rachel Prochoroff Castanheira
Coordenadora de arte	Karina Monteiro
Assistente de arte	Marilia Vilela
	Tomás Troppmair
Coordenadora de iconografia	Maria do Céu Pires Passuello
Assistente de iconografia	Adriana Neves
	Wilson de Castilho
Ilustrações	Lie Kobayashi
Produção editorial	Paula Calviello
Produção gráfica	José Antônio Ferraz
Assistente de produção gráfica	Eliane M. M. Ferreira
Projeto gráfico e capa	Departamento de arte IBEP
Editoração eletrônica	Formato Comunicação

CIP-BRASIL. CATALOGAÇÃO-NA-FONTE
SINDICATO NACIONAL DOS EDITORES DE LIVROS, RJ

L32i

Laporta, Edgar
    Inglês : 9º ano / Edgar Laporta. - 1.ed. - São Paulo : IBEP, 2012.
    il. ; 28 cm.   (Eu gosto mais)

    ISBN 978-85-342-3447-4 (aluno) - 978-85-342-3451-1 (mestre)

    1. Língua inglesa - Estudo e ensino (Ensino fundamental). I. Título. II. Série.

12-6213   CDD: 372.6521
                                                                         CDU: 373.3.016=111

28.08.12   05.09.12   038548

1ª Reimpressão - 2014
1ª edição - São Paulo - 2012
Todos os direitos reservados

Av. Alexandre Mackenzie, 619 - Jaguaré
São Paulo - SP - 05322-000 - Brasil - Tel.: (11) 2799-7799
www.editoraibep.com.br   editoras@ibep-nacional.com.br

CTP, Impressão e Acabamento IBEP Gráfica
45120

Apresentação

O inglês é um idioma de grande importância no mundo globalizado de hoje. Está presente em nossa vida diária, na TV, no cinema, na Internet, nas músicas, nos livros, nas revistas etc.

Há muito tempo, tornou-se um dos principais meios de comunicação no turismo, no comércio mundial, nas competições esportivas, nos congressos sobre ciência e tecnologia, nos meios diplomáticos, nos encontros de líderes mundiais etc. Por isso, cada vez mais pessoas estudam e falam inglês.

Com o objetivo de despertar em você o gosto pelo idioma inglês, tivemos a preocupação de abordar textos variados e que se relacionam com sua vida.

As atividades de interpretação dos textos levam você a ler e reler o texto para encontrar as respostas adequadas às perguntas.

Sempre que você tiver alguma dificuldade em descobrir o sentido de palavras ou expressões do texto, lembre-se de que há no final do livro o vocabulário geral para ajudá-lo.

As noções de gramática são apresentadas na seção *Learn this* de forma simples e abreviada. Logo a seguir, você vai treiná-las com exercícios rápidos e simples.

Participe ativamente das aulas e aproveite esta oportunidade para aprender inglês.

O autor

Sumário

Lesson 1 – Greetings: How are you? What's your name? 7
Dialogue: *China, a booming economy* 7
    Text comprehension 8
    Learn this 9
    Activities 9
    Learn this 10
    Activities 11
    Learn this 12
    Activities 13
    Fun time 14

Lesson 2 – Personal pronouns/ object pronouns 15
Dialogue: *I lost my documents* 15
    Text comprehension 16
    Learn this 16
    Activities 17
    Review 18
    Listen and write – dictation 19
    Fun time 19

Lesson 3 – Position of the object pronoun 20
Dialogue: *At the doctor's* 20
    Text comprehension 21
    Learn this 21
    Activities 22

Lesson 4 – Indefinite pronouns (some, any) 23
Dialogues: *Some time, some coins?* 23
    Text comprehension 24
    Learn this 24
    Activities 25
    Fun time 26

Lesson 5 – Prepositions of time and place: in, on, at 27
Dialogues: *Talking about birthday and address* 27
    Text comprehension 28
    Review 28
    Learn this 29
    Activities 29
    Fun time 31
    Review 31

Lesson 6 – Future tense (affirmative, interrogative and negative forms) 34
Dialogue: *What will you do?* 34
    Text comprehension 35
    Learn this 36
    Activities 36
    Review 38
    Fun time 41

Lesson 7 – Conditional tense (affirmative – negative – interrogative) contracted forms 43

Dialogue: *What would you do if you won in the lottery?*..........43

   Text comprehension 44

   Learn this 44

   Activities 45

   Fun time 47

Lesson 8 – Question tags 48

Dialogue: *At the airport customs* 48

   Text comprehension 49

   Learn this 49

   Activities 50

Lesson 9 – Comparative of equality, superiority and inferiority 52

Text: *Which is more beautiful?* 52

   Learn this 54

   Activities 55

   Review 56

   Fun time 57

Lesson 10 – Superlative degree of adjectives 59

Text: *The Burj Al Arab* 59

Text: *Iguaçu Falls* 60

   Text comprehension 60

   Learn this 61

   Activities 62

   Let's sing 63

Lesson 11 – Present perfect tense 64

Text: *Technology* 64

   Text comprehension 65

   Learn this 65

   Activities 67

   Fun time 70

Lesson 12 – Active voice and passive voice 71

Dialogue: *The first Americans* 71

   Text comprehension 72

   Learn this 73

   Activities 74

   Review 75

   Fun time 77

Lesson 13 – Indefinite adjectives and pronouns 78

Text: *Education* 78

   Text comprehension 79

   Learn this 79

   Activities 81

Lesson 14 – Adverbs of time, frequency, manner, place, intensity, negation and affirmation 84

Text: *Proverbs*..84

    Text comprehension 85

    Learn this 85

    Activities 87

    Let's sing 88

Lesson 15 – Relative pronouns 89

Text: *Thanksgiving Day*
(Dia de Ação de Graças) 89

    Text comprehension 90

    Learn this 91

    Activities 91

    Review 93

    Fun time 95

Lesson 16 – Also/too/either/neither ... 96

Text: *I live on a farm* 96

    Text comprehension 97

    Learn this 97

    Activities 98

Capítulo 17 – Gerund after prepositions and some verbs 100

Dialogue: *Don't waste water!* 100

    Text comprehension 101

    Learn this 102

    Activities 103

    Fun time 104

Additional texts 105

List of irregular verbs 113

General vocabulary 114

Lesson 1

GREETINGS: HOW ARE YOU? WHAT'S YOUR NAME?

China, a booming economy

Brazilian:	Hi!
Chinese:	Hi!
Brazilian:	What's your name?
Chinese:	My name is Shaofu. And what's your name?
Brazilian:	My name is Toni. Where are you from?
Chinese:	I'm from Xangai, China.
Brazilian:	Do you speak Portuguese?
Chinese:	Yes, I do, but I prefer to speak English. And you, do you speak Mandarin?
Brazilian:	No, I don't. I think it's a very difficult language... But can you tell me something about your country?
Chinese:	Sure! China is the most populous country in the world. There are about 1,300,000,000 (one bilion and three hundred million) people. Chinese economy is booming. China produces everything: from a small pin or clip to heavy machines at very low price, so it's impossible for the other countries to compete with China's products.
Brazilian:	And that's the problem! Chinese products invade our country and take away the jobs of so many Brazilian workers!
Chinese:	I'm sorry. But China is not only a rich economy. It has one of the most ancient cultures in the world. In recent years Chinese culture has changed greatly. You can see young people dressed like American teens and chatting with their friends on their cell phones

Did you know?

- China is the third largest country in the world.
  (first: Russia; second: Canada; third: China; fourth: The United States; fifth: Brazil)
- Population: China has got about one billion and three hundred million inhabitants.
- Language: the dialect Mandarin is the official language of China.

The Forbidden City in Beijing (China).
The magnificent **Forbidden City** is the largest and the best-
-preserved Imperial Palace complex in the world. It was the residence of emperors. It has about 8.000 (eight thousand) rooms.
Why **Forbidden**? Because no one could enter or leave it without the Emperor's permission.

The **Great Wall** is one of the "Eight wonders of the World" and the longest wall in the world. It measures about 6,000 kilometers long. The wall was designed to protect China from its enemies.

TEXT COMPREHENSION

1 Where is Shaofu from?
_____

2 Where is Toni from?
_____

3 What languages does Shaofu speak?
_____

4 What languages does Toni speak?
_____

5 What is the main language used in China?
_____

6 Is the Mandarin language easy or difficult?
_____

7 How many people are there in China?
_____

8 The goods or products exported by China are:

( ) very expensive ( ) very cheap ( ) neither cheap nor expensive

9 Complete the answer with these words:

> jobs - goods - Chinese - job - workers

How can China industry prejudice Brazilian workers?

Because the _____ imported from China are not produced by Brazilian _____ and for this reason many Brazilian workers can't get a _____ or are dismissed from their _____.

Brazilian manufactures prefer to import _____ goods due to the low prices.

LEARN THIS

1. **Interrogative form – auxiliary verbs**
   Para se obter a forma interrogativa com verbos auxiliares, basta inverter o sujeito com o verbo:

   China is the most populous country in the world.
   Is China the most populous country in the world?
   You can tell something about your country.
   Can you tell something about your country?

2. **Negative form – auxiliary verbs**
   Para se obter a forma negativa com verbos auxiliares, basta colocar **not** após o verbo:

   His name is Bob.
   His name is not Bob.
   I can speak Mandarin.
   I cannot speak Mandarin. (I can't speak Mandarin.)
   He was a famous scientist.
   He was not a famous scientist.

ACTIVITIES

1 Change to the interrogative form:

a) China is a populous country. _____

b) She is a Chinese girl. _____

c) They can speak Mandarin. _____

d) Mandarin is a difficult language. _____

e) Confucius was born in China. _____

f) Confucius was a famous philosopher. _____

g) Chinese society is changing. _____

8 Change to the negative form:

a) He was a famous singer. _____

b) His favorite sport is tennis. _____

c) They were my friends. _____

d) English is a difficult language. _____

e) I can speak Mandarin. _____

LEARN THIS

1. **Interrogative form – common verbs: do, does, did**
   Com verbos não auxiliares, são usadas as formas **do** e **does** para interrogar no presente do indicativo e **did** no tempo passado:

   You speak English.
   Do you speak English?
   She speaks English.
   Does she speak English?
   He changed his phone number.
   Did he change his phone number?

2. **Negative form – common verbs: do not (don't), does not (doesn't) and did not (didn't).**
   Com verbos não auxiliares, empregam-se as formas **do not** e **does not** no tempo presente e **did not** no tempo passado para a forma negativa:

   I speak English.
   I do not speak English.
   I don't speak English.
   She speaks Mandarin.
   She does not speak Mandarin.
   She doesn't speak Mandarin.
   China products invaded our country.
   China products did not invade our country.
   China products didn't invade our country.

ACTIVITIES

1 Change to the interrogative form:

a) **You like Geography.**   **Do you like Geography?**

b) She likes History. _____

c) They know China. _____

d) Chinese society changed greatly. _____

e) The Chinese invented the paper and the fireworks. _____

f) China made a large progress in technology. _____

2 Change to the negative form:

a) **I like Geography.**   **I do not like Geography. (I don´t like Geography.)**

b) She likes Science. _____

c) I speak Japanese. _____

d) Brazilian society changed greatly. _____

e) She likes to read. _____

f) They admire our country. _____

3 Change to the interrogative form:

a) **The students went to school by bus.**   **Did the students go to school by bus?**

b) The lesson began at eight o´clock. _____

c) Chris sold her old car. _____

d) You drank two bottles of water. _____

e) Many girls play soccer nowadays. _____

f) John lost his keys. _____

g) They told the truth to the teacher. _____

h) You learned many things about China. _____

i) The children ate all the chocolate. _____

j) My parents paid the bill. _____

k) She went to the dentist´s. _____

4 Change to the negative form:

a) **She went to the doctor´s.**
She did not go to the doctor´s.
(She didn´t go to the doctor´s.)

b) Robin gave a present to me.
_____
_____

c) I like History.
_____
_____

d) She dances well.
_____
_____

e) We found the documents.
_____
_____

f) I understand you.
_____
_____

g) She understands me.
_____
_____

h) They understood me.
_____
_____

LEARN THIS

1. **Too** significa também. É usado em final de frases afirmativas.
   I like fruit. My friend likes fruit, too.
   (Eu gosto de frutas. Meu amigo também gosta de frutas.)
2. **Either** significa também não. É usado em final de frases negativas.
   I don't like fish. My friend doesn´t like fish either.
   (Eu não gosto de peixe. Meu amigo também não gosta de peixe.)

3. **Too** antes de adjetivos e quantificadores tem função intensificadora.

   too easy = fácil demais

   The lesson is too easy. (A lição é fácil demais.)

   too much = demais

   There is too much sugar in my coffee. (Tem açúcar demais em meu café.)

   He sleeps too much. (Ele dorme demais.)

   Observe o emprego de "**too much**":

   LEMON FACES

   Is your lemonade fine?

   Look at these lemon faces!

> **Word bank**
> **sugar:** açúcar
> **water:** água
> **lemon:** limão
> **lemonade:** limonada
> **face:** rosto

Too much lemon!

Too much water!

Too much sugar!

Perfect!

ACTIVITIES

1 Complete the sentences with too or either:

a) I like to read. Mary likes to read, _____

b) I live in Rio. My parents live in Rio, _____

c) I don´t like football. Mary doesn´t like football _____

d) The bus doesn´t stop here. The train doesn´t stop here _____

e) I don´t drink coffee. I don´t drink tea _____

f) I help my friends. I help my family, _____

2 Complete with too:

a) This lemonade has _____ much sugar!

b) This juice has _____ much water!

c) This salad has _____ much salt!

thirteen **13**

FUN TIME

1 Look at the list of the irregular verbs at the end of this book and write the past tense of the verbs below in the crosswords:

1. to begin
2. to drink
3. to speak
4. to tell
5. to sell
6. to teach
7. to find
8. to go
9. to give
10. to meet
11. to write
12. to know
13. to see
14. to buy
15. to understand
16. to lose
17. to pay

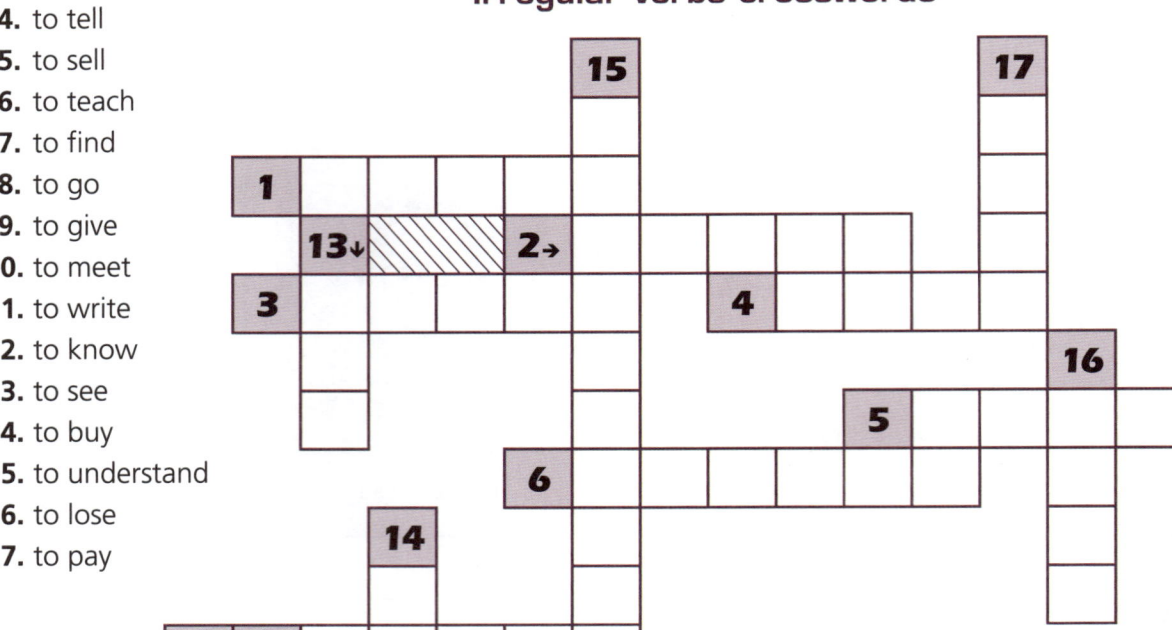

Irregular verbs crosswords

Lesson 2
PERSONAL PRONOUNS/ OBJECT PRONOUNS

I lost my documents

Paul: Can I help you, Monica?
Monica: No, you can't help me, Paul.
Paul: Why not? I'm your friend and I want to help you...
Monica: Well...
I'm worried because I lost my documents.
I looked for them everywhere but I didn't find them.
Paul: Where were you yesterday?
Monica: I was at the club and at the supermarket.
Paul, wait a moment. My cell phone is ringing...
Secretary: Are you Monica?
Monica: Yes, I'm Monica.
Secretary: Somebody found your documents at the snack bar of the club. Can you get them here?
Monica: Sure! Thank you!
I'm going to get them right now!

TEXT COMPREHENSION

1 Who wants to help Monica?
_____

2 Who is worried?
_____

3 Why is Monica worried?
_____

4 Where did Monica look for her documents?
_____

5 Where was Monica yesterday?
_____

6 Where were Monica's documents?
_____

7 Who found Monica's documents?
( ) The secretary of the club   ( ) an unknown person   ( ) Paul

8 Who telephoned to say that the documents were at the snack bar of the club?
_____

9 Monica is going to get the documents
( ) tomorrow   ( ) right now

LEARN THIS

Personal pronouns

Subject pronouns	Object pronouns
I	me (me)
you	you (te, você, lhe, o, a)
he	him (lhe, o)
she	her (lhe, a)
it	it (lhe, o, a)
we	us (nos)
you	you (vos, vocês, lhes, os, as)
they	them (lhes, os, as)

Observe alguns exemplos:

- **Can I help you?** (Posso ajudar você?) (Posso ajudá-lo?)
- **You can't help me.** (Você não pode ajudar-me.)
- **You can save him.** (Você pode salvá-lo.)
- **I found it in the drawer.** (Eu o encontrei na gaveta.)
- **I saw them yesterday.** (Eu os vi ontem.)
- **Come with us.** (Venha conosco.)

ACTIVITIES

1 Substitute the underlined nouns by object pronouns:

a) Mary likes <u>John</u>.
   Mary likes him.

b) John likes <u>Mary</u>.
   _____

c) We like <u>John and Mary</u>.
   _____

d) Look <u>at the birds</u>.
   _____

e) The book is with <u>Mr. Brown</u>.
   _____

f) Did you find <u>the key</u>?
   _____

g) I visited <u>my friends</u> yesterday.
   _____

h) Did you write to <u>John</u>?
   _____

i) Did you telephone <u>Jane</u>?
   _____

j) Did you like <u>the film</u>?
   _____

2 Answer negatively:

a) **Did you see Peter?**   **No, I didn't see him.**

b) Do you know Mary?   _____

c) Did you read the book?   _____

d) Did you write to your parents? _____

e) Did you buy the house?   _____

3 Change to the plural form:

a) **I want to visit him.**   **We want to visit them.**

b) She saw me.   _____

c) He found it in the park.   _____

d) Did you meet him?   _____

e) I like her.   _____

REVIEW

1 Translate

Somebody found your documents. Can you get them at the snack bar?
_____

2 Answer negatively:
a) Does Paul help Liz? _____
b) Does Liz speak Mandarin? _____
c) Did the secretary lose her documents? _____

3 Answer the questions:
a) How many inhabitants are there in Brazil? _____
b) Is China a small or a large country? _____

4 Change to the interrogative form:
a) You can speak Japanese. _____
b) Japanese is a difficult language. _____
c) They are from China. _____
d) She likes English. _____
e) They admire your country. _____

5 Change to the negative form:
a) She likes fish. _____
b) I speak German. _____
c) The show began at 7. _____
d) We paid the bill. _____
e) She went to the club. _____
f) I understand you. _____
g) He teaches Science. _____
h) She told me the truth. _____

6 Translate:

Don´t be selfish! Pass the ball to me.
_____

7 Change the underlined nouns into object pronouns:
a) The keys are with <u>Mr Garfield</u>.
_____

b) Look at the <u>airplanes</u>.
_____

c) I visited <u>Mary</u> yesterday.
_____

d) Did you like the <u>ice cream</u>?
_____

18 eigtheen

8 Write the past tense of these irregular verbs:

a) to go: _____
b) to see: _____
c) to find: _____
d) to buy: _____
e) to lose: _____

f) to give: _____
g) to sell: _____
h) to tell: _____
i) to pay: _____
j) to begin: _____

LISTEN AND WRITE – DICTATION

Listen to the teacher and complete the text:

– _____ I _____ you?

– No, you _____.

– _____ not? _____ your friend.

– _____. I'm _____ I _____ my documents.

– Were _____ at the _____?

– Yes _____.

– Let's call the _____ and found section _____.

FUN TIME

No words

Lesson 3

POSITION OF THE OBJECT PRONOUN

At the doctor's

Kate: Last week I went to the doctor's because I had a headache.
Raimond: What did the doctor prescribe to you?
Kate: He prescribed me a pain killer.
Raimond: Did you take the pain killer last night?
Kate: Yes, I did.
Raimond: Do you feel better today?
Kate: Oh, yes! Last night I slept for 7 hours without interruption.
Raimond: Is the pain killer expensive?
Kate: I don't know. The doctor gave it to me.

TEXT COMPREHENSION

1. Where did Kate go last week?
   _____

2. Why did she go to the doctor's?
   _____

3. What did the doctor prescribe to Kate?
   _____

4. Did Kate take the pain killer last night?
   _____

5. Does Kate feel better today?
   _____

6. How many hours did Kate sleep last night?
   _____

7. Did Kate buy the pain killer?
   _____

8. Why?
   _____

LEARN THIS

Object pronouns

1. Posição dos pronomes na frase
   Observe os exemplos a e b e compare-os:
   a) **Give him this shirt**. (Dê para ele esta camisa.)
   b) **Give this shirt to him**. (Dê esta camisa para ele.)
   No exemplo a, o objeto indireto (**him**) vem antes do objeto direto (**this shirt**).
   No exemplo b, o objeto direto (**this shirt**) vem antes do objeto indireto (**him**). Neste caso temos de usar a preposição **to**.
   Regra: Quando o objeto indireto vem depois do objeto direto, usa-se a preposição **to**.

2. Use o pronome objeto depois de preposições.
   Exemplo:
   I need to buy a present for them. (Eu preciso comprar um presente para eles.)
   I bought a shirt for him and a blouse for her. (Eu comprei uma camisa para ele e uma blusa para ela.)

ACTIVITIES

1 Change the position of the object pronoun. Put the indirect object at the end of the sentence:

a) **Give her the ball.**
   Give the ball to her.

b) Give him the money.
   _____

c) I showed him the book.
   _____

d) I sent her a letter.
   _____

e) She sent me a telegram.
   _____

f) I brought her flowers.
   _____

g) Lend me a pencil!
   _____

h) I delivered them the goods.
   _____

2 Change the position of the indirect object:

a) I showed the city to him.
   _____

b) She gave a present to him.
   _____

c) He sent a letter to her.
   _____

d) She told a secret to him.
   _____

e) They showed the way to me.
   _____

f) We took some money to them.
   _____

g) You gave the key to me.
   _____

h) I delivered the message to him.
   _____

3 Choose the correct pronoun:

a) I want to speak to _____. (they – them)

b) Do you know _____? (he – him)

c) I went there but _____ was not at home. (he – him)

d) I can go with _____. (he – him)

e) A famous French king said:
   "After _____, the deluge". (I – me)

f) Among _____ there is a traitor. (we – us)

g) She was sitting behind _____. (he – him)

h) I know all about _____. (they – them)

i) Don´t forget _____ on my birthday. (I – me)

j) Don´t leave _____ alone. (she – her)

Lesson 4
INDEFINITE PRONOUNS (SOME, ANY)

Some time, some coins?

Clerk: Excuse me, do you have some time to listen to me?
President: No, I don't have any time for you now. I'm very busy! Come later, please.

Beggar: Excuse me, do you have some coins to buy a lunch? I am so hungry!
Woman: I'm sorry. I don't have any coins, but take these biscuits.

Mother: Chris, I'm at the supermarket. Please look in the fridge and check whether there is some cheese and milk there...
Chris: Wait a moment, mom. There is not any cheese but there are some quarts of milk.

TEXT COMPREHENSION

1 Look at the text and at the first picture and answer:

a) Does the president listen to the clerk?
_____

b) The president doesn't listen to the clerk because
( ) he is sick ( ) he is impolite ( ) he is busy

2 Look at the text and at the second picture and answer:

a) A poor hungry man is asking a woman to give him:
( ) some food ( ) some coins ( ) some clothes

3 Look at the text and at the third picture and answer:

a) Where is Chris' mother?
_____

b) Why is she calling Chris?
_____

c) Is there any cheese in the fridge?
_____

d) Is there any milk in the fridge?
_____

LEARN THIS

Indefinite pronouns (some, any)

Some é usado em frases afirmativas e **any** em frases interrogativas e negativas.

Observe os exemplos:

I want some mangoes.	(Eu quero algumas mangas.)
We don´t have any mangoes today.	(Nós não temos nenhuma manga hoje.)
There is some milk in the refrigerator.	(Há algum leite na geladeira.)
Is there any milk in the refrigerator?	(Há algum leite na geladeira?)
No, there is not any milk in the refrigerator.	(Não, não há nenhum leite na geladeira.)

Observação

Podemos usar **some** em frases interrogativas quando esperamos resposta positiva.
- **Do you have some money?**
- **Yes, I have some money.**

ACTIVITIES

1 Look at the example and answer the questions:

a) cheese / refrigerator (No)
   Is there any cheese in the refrigerator?
   No, there is not any cheese in the refrigerator.

b) eggs / in the box (Yes)
   Are there any eggs in the box?
   Yes, there are some eggs in the box.

c) butter / on the table (No)
   _____
   _____

d) sugar / in the coffee (Yes)
   _____
   _____

e) meat / in the refrigerator (Yes)
   _____
   _____

f) potatoes / in the basket (Yes)
   _____
   _____

2 Change to the interrogative form:

a) **You bought some books yesterday.**
   Did you buy any books yesterday?

b) There is some sugar in the sugar bowl.
   _____

c) You found some difficulty in the lesson.
   _____

3 Change to the negative form:

a) I have some money.
   _____

b) There are some eggs in the nest.
   _____

c) I found my keys in the drawer.
   _____

d) There is some money in his pocket.
   _____

twenty-five **25**

4. Complete the sentences with **some** or **any**:

a) I saw _____ good programs on TV tonight.

b) Can you lend me _____ money?

c) To prepare this cake we need _____ eggs and _____ sugar.

d) I gave him _____ money.

e) Did you find _____ difficulty in this lesson?

f) No, I didn´t find _____ difficulty.

g) Did you drink _____ beer yesterday?

h) No, I didn´t drink _____ beer yesterday.

i) I need _____ time to finish this work.

FUN TIME

What falls down day and night and never gets hurt?
_____

What an intelligent dog! It turns on the alarm whenever a thief tries to enter the house.

26 twenty-six

Lesson 5

PREPOSITIONS OF TIME AND PLACE: IN, ON, AT

Talking about birthday and address

Paul: When were you born, Liz?
Liz: I was born in 1999. (nineteen ninety-nine)
Paul: What month were you born?
Liz: I was born in December.
Paul: What day of December were you born?
Liz: I was born on the second day of December.
Paul: And what day of the week were you born?
Liz: I was born on a Sunday.
Paul: What time were you born?
Liz: I was born at 7 o´clock.
Liz: Where do you live, Paul?
Paul: I live in Brazil.
Liz: What city?
Paul: I live in Salvador.
Liz: What is your address?
Paul: I live on Caxias Street.
Liz: Number?
Paul: I live at 26 Caxias Street.

TEXT COMPREHENSION

1 Liz was born in 1999.
How old is she now?
_____

2 What month was Liz born?
Liz was born
( ) in March   ( ) in June   ( ) in December

3 What time of the day was Liz born?
_____

4 What day of the week was Liz born?
Liz was born
( ) on a Monday   ( ) on a Wednesday
( ) on a Tuesday   ( ) on a Sunday

5 What country does Paul live in?
_____

6 What city does Paul live in?
_____

7 What is Paul address?
_____

REVIEW

Months of the year
January
February
March
April
May
June
July
August
September
October
November
December

Days of the week
Sunday
Monday
Tuesday
Wednesday
Thursday
Friday
Saturday

Note: write the names of the months and the days of the week with capital letter.

twenty-eigth

LEARN THIS

Prepositions in, on, at:

Observe o emprego das preposições **in**, **on**, **at** em relação a tempo e lugar:

Time

I was born
- **in 1970.** (ano)
- **in December.** (mês)
- **on a Sunday.** (dia da semana)
- **on the 27th of December 1970.** (data)
- **at 7 o'clock** (hora)

Place

I live
- **in Brazil.** (país)
- **in São Paulo.** (cidade)
- **on Brazil Avenue.** (rua)
- **at 27 Siriema Street.** (nº de rua)

Observações

1. Para grandes unidades (ano, mês, país, cidade), empregamos a preposição **in**.
Para unidades médias (dias da semana, datas, ruas) usamos a preposição **on**.
Para unidades pequenas (horas, nº de rua), usamos **at**.

2. Leitura de datas.
Exemplo: 27 December 1970 (the twenty-seventh of December, nineteen seventy.)

ACTIVITIES

1 Com base no diálogo entre Liz e Paul e nos conteúdos da página anterior, os alunos, em duplas, perguntam e respondem sobre seus aniversários e endereços:

Time

a) When were you born?

   I was born in (year) _____

b) What month were you born?

   I was born in (month) _____

c) What day of (month) were you born?

   I was born on _____

d) What day of the week were you born?

   I was born on a (day) _____

e) What time were you born?

   I was born at _____

Place

f) Where do you live?

   I live in (country) _____

g) What city?

   I live in (city) _____

h) What street?

   I live on (street) _____

i) What number?

   I live at (number) (street) _____

2 Insert the correct preposition:

a) I live _____ Rodrigues Alves Street.

b) Mariana lives _____ 29 Juriti Street.

c) Giovana was born _____ Italy but now she lives _____ Brazil.

d) I was born _____ Rio Grande do Sul, and you?

   I was born _____ Rio Grande do Norte.

e) When is your birthday?

   My birthday is _____ the second of April.

f) What is your address?

   I live _____ 75 Safira Street.

3 Answer the questions. Look at the model:

a) What time do you get up? (7 o´clock)   I get up at seven o´clock.

b) What time do you go to school? (8 o´clock)

_____

c) Where were you born? (Brazil)

_____

d) Where were you born? (Recife)

_____

e) When were you born? (1975)

_____

f) Where do you live? (United States)

_____

g) Where do you live? (Florida Street)

_____

h) What is your address? (24 Florida Street)

_____

FUN TIME

1 Opposites

Write the opposites. There is a word without opposite. What is it?

It is _____.

Make use of this list:

buy – finish – beautiful alive – in front of – first – go get up – near – fat – tall forget – good – receive

behind	_____	last	_____
dead	_____	short	_____
give	_____	thin	_____
sell	_____	blue	_____
begin	_____	far	_____
ugly	_____	bad	_____
go to bed	_____	remember	_____
come	_____		

REVIEW

1 Fill in the blanks with the correct pronoun:
a) She sits near _____. (me, I)
b) I know both of _____. (they, them)
c) I am not satisfied with _____. (he, him)
d) Where are _____? (them, they)
e) What is the matter with _____? (he, him)
f) I gave the book to _____. (her, she)
g) This present is for _____. (she, her)
h) I saw _____ on the bus. (he, him)
i) He goes to the movies with _____. (she, her)
j) The pen belongs to _____. (he, him)
k) We waited for _____ last night. (they, them)
l) I understand _____ very well. (he, him)
m) I gave _____ some money. (she, her)

2 Fill in the blanks with some or any:
a) There are _____ flowers in the vase.
b) There are _____ pupils in the class.
c) We don´t have _____ money.
d) There aren´t _____ toys in the box.
e) He didn´t find _____ friends at the party.
f) There weren´t _____ vegetables in the fridge.
g) The postman delivered _____ letters.

thirty-one **31**

h) Are there _____ pens in the drawer?
i) No, there aren´t _____ pens in the drawer.
j) Is there _____ water in the bottle?
k) No, there isn´t _____ water in the bottle.

3 Change the position of the object pronoun:

a) **Lend me your book.**
   Lend your book to me.

b) Give her the present.
   _____

c) Send a letter to them.
   _____

d) Peter delivered the merchandise to them.
   _____

e) She told them a story.
   _____

f) Don´t tell him lies.
   _____

g) We told the truth to her.
   _____

4 Change to the negative form:

a) **There is some money in the drawer.**
   There is not any money in the drawer.

b) **I bought some sweets.**
   I didn't buy any sweets.

c) There are some men in the house.
   _____

d) There are some birds in the tree.
   _____

e) I have some time to study English.
   _____

f) There are some oranges in the basket.
   _____

g) I found some mistakes in the dictation.
   _____

THIS VOCABULARY MAY HELP YOU

cupboard: armário de cozinha
bathroom: banheiro
chair: cadeira
bed: cama
rug: capacho
chimney: chaminé
curtains: cortina
kitchen: cozinha
bookcase: estante de livros
stove: fogão
refrigerator: geladeira
wardrobe: guarda-roupa

window: janela
lamp: lâmpada
wash-basin: lavabo
table: mesa
sink: pia
door: porta
picture: quadro
radio: rádio
living room: sala de estar
dining room: sala de jantar
sofa: sofá
carpet: tapete

5 Complete the crossword on the next page according to these pictures:

A house crossword

Lesson 6

Future tense (affirmative, interrogative and negative forms)

What will you do?

Reporter: What's your name?
Lucy: My name is Lucy.
Reporter: What will you do in the future?
Lucy: I intend to be a doctor. As a doctor I will take care of people's health. I will try to save many lives.
Reporter: Very good.
Reporter: What's your name?
Edward: My name is Edward.
Reporter: Edward, what will you do in the future?
Edward: I will be a baker! I like bread. I like to cook.
Reporter: But as a baker will you produce only bread?
Edward: Oh, no! I will produce all sorts of cakes, biscuits, toasts, ice creams, etc. My bakery will be the best in the city!
Reporter: Congratulations!

Reporter: What's your name?
Paul: My name is Paul.
Reporter: What will you be when you grow up?
Paul: I intend to be a teacher.
Reporter: A teacher? But teacher's have to be very patient.
Paul: It doesn't matter! My aim is to teach many Brazilian teenagers to become responsible citizens, transform this country and end social injustice.
Reporter: Excellent!
Reporter: What's your name?
Carol: My name is Carol.
Reporter: What will you do when you grow up?
Carol: I will be a veterinarian. I like animals. As a veterinarian I will give medical treatment to sick animals. I will vaccinate them to protect them from diseases.
Reporter: Which kinds of animals will you take care?
Carol: Specially domestic animals: dogs, cats, pigs, hens, cows, horses, goats, sheep, rabbits...
Reporter: Good luck in your occupation!

TEXT COMPREHENSION

1. Who intends to be a doctor? _____
2. What will Lucy do as a doctor? _____
3. Who wants to be a veterinarian? _____
4. Does Carol like animals? _____
5. What will Carol do as a veterinarian? _____
6. Which kinds of animals will Carol take care? _____

7. Who intends to be a teacher? _____
8. Teacher's usually have to be.
   ( ) nice   ( ) patient   ( ) irritated
9. What is Paul's aim as a teacher?

10 Who likes bread and intends to be a baker?

_____

11 Will Edward's bakery produce only bread?

_____

LEARN THIS

Future tense

Para se formar o futuro, em inglês, basta colocar o auxiliar **will** antes da forma básica do verbo (infinitivo sem o **to**): **He will find a job**. (Ele encontrará um emprego.)
Na forma interrogativa basta inverter o sujeito e o verbo: **Will she go?** (Ela irá?)
Na negativa coloca-se **not** depois de **will**: **She will not go**. (Ela não irá.) Pode-se usar a forma contraída **won't**: **She won't go**. (Ela não irá)
Observe a conjugação do verbo **to find** no futuro:

Affirmative form	Contracted form
I will find (eu encontrarei)	I'll find
You will find (você encontrará)	You'll find
He will find (ele encontrará)	He'll find
She will find (ela encontrará)	She'll find
It will find (ele/ela encontrará)	It'll find
We will find (nós encontraremos)	We'll find
You will find (vocês encontrarão)	You'll find
They will find (eles/elas encontrarão)	They'll find

ACTIVITIES

1 Write in the future tense:
a) **She knows her future.**
   She will know her future.

b) They consult a fortune-teller.

_____

_____

c) Magnus predicts the future.

_____

_____

d) She doesn't meet her boyfriend at night.

_____

_____

2 Follow the pattern:
a) I – leave – São Paulo – next – week
   I will leave São Paulo next week.
b) You – work – a big factory
   _____

c) She – be – a very happy woman
   _____

3 Write in the contracted form:
a) **I will be home at seven.**
   I'll be home at seven.
b) You will return next month.
   _____

c) He will travel next summer.
   _____

d) They will come next week.
   _____

e) We will leave Rio in winter.
   _____

4 Change to the interrogative form:
a) **Peter will get a good job.**
   Will Peter get a good job?
b) She will be very happy.
   _____

c) Jane will marry her teacher.
   _____

d) Charles will buy a motorcycle.
   _____

5 Change to the negative form (using will not and won't):
a) **He will predict the future.**
   He will not predict the future. He won't predict the future.
b) She will meet you on Sunday morning.
   _____

thirty-seven **37**

c) I will go out with her.

___

d) They will work on Sundays.

___

REVIEW

1 Substitution table.

In your copybook, write questions and then answer them substituting the underlined words by:

toy, bicycle, guitar, watch, book, table, turkey, donkey, etc.

a) **What did you buy yesterday?**
   I bought a car.

b) **What did you buy yesterday?**
   I bought a toy.

2 Change to the interrogative form:
   a) They are sitting at the round table.
   ___

   b) They like coffee.
   ___

   c) She loves you.
   ___

   d) They invited the social assistant.
   ___

   e) The class began at 7.
   ___

   f) You sold the old car.
   ___

   g) They understood the lesson.
   ___

3 Change to the negative form (full form and contracted form):
   a) **The food is good.**
      The food is not good.
      The food isn't good.

38 thirty-eigth

b) She was at home a week ago.

c) They get a lot of money.

d) She lost the key.

e) They told the truth.

f) She invited me.

g) They helped me.

4 Change to the future tense (full and short forms):
a) She comes on Tuesday.

b) I stay at home.

c) I travel next month.

5 Change to the interrogative form:
a) She will come tomorrow.

b) You will stay at home.

c) The class will begin at 7.

6 Change to the negative form:
a) We will leave tomorrow.

b) I will buy a new car.

c) I will work tomorrow.

thirty-nine **39**

7 Look at the pictures and the model and do the same:

a) Mary – to cross the street
Mary is going to cross the street.

She is crossing the street.

She has just crossed the street.

b) Jane – to eat an apple

c) Bob – to shut the door

d) Jim – to drink a glass of milk

e) Nancy – to buy some flowers

FUN TIME

1 Complete the crosswords:

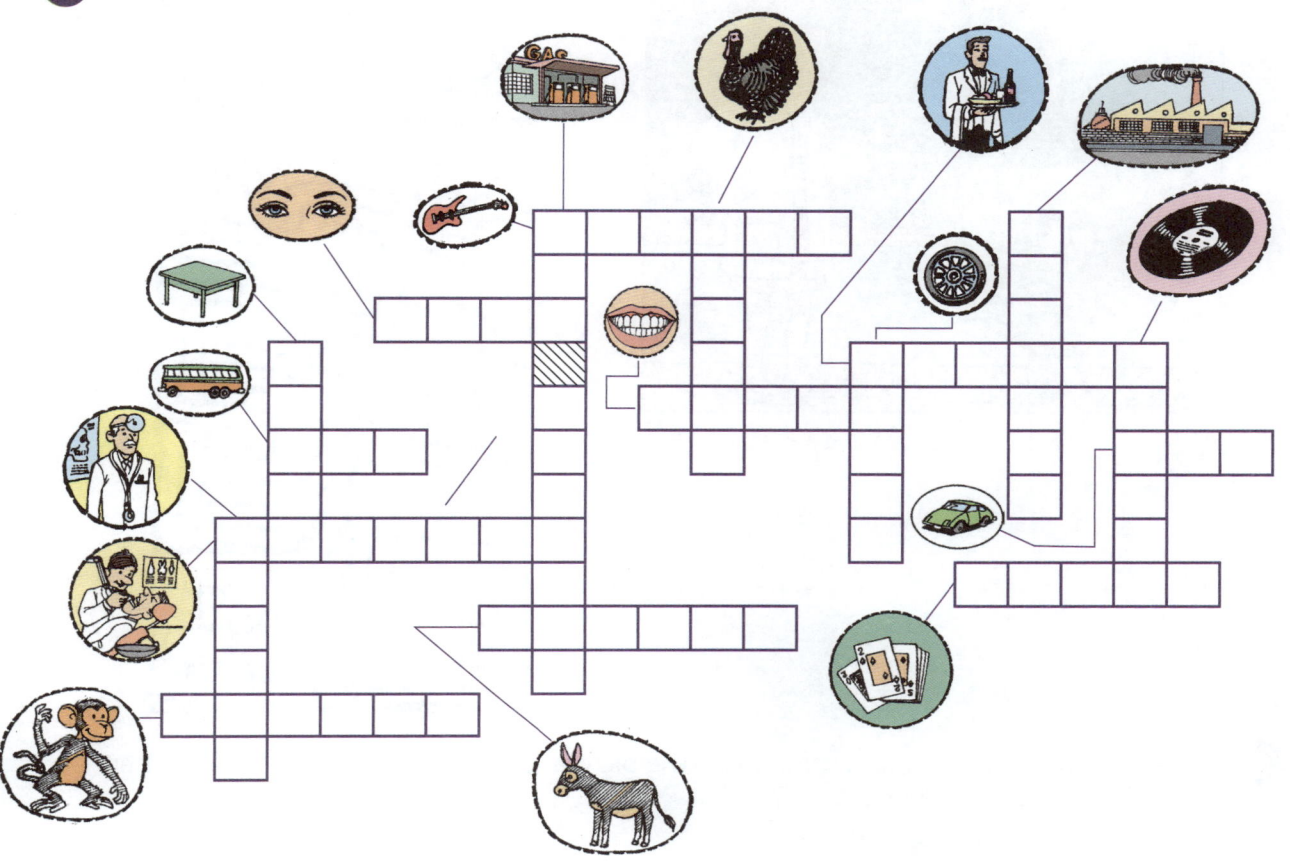

Word Hunt

2 Find the days of the week:

B	H	A	C	S	E	S	A	T	U	R	D	A	Y	Q	O	S	T
L	J	V	T	U	E	S	D	A	Y	B	A	H	A	I	R	G	F
W	E	D	N	E	S	D	A	Y	N	T	H	U	R	S	D	A	Y
Y	T	R	E	Q	F	R	I	D	A	Y	F	B	V	C	X	Z	T
M	B	N	S	U	N	D	A	Y	R	U	O	Y	R	D	S	Q	T
Q	F	B	V	C	X	Z	M	O	N	D	A	Y	R	D	E	A	W

forty-one **41**

3 What has a big head but cannot think?

Two plus two is...

_____

4 What's the right way?

Help the hen to find its young chickens.

5 A little girl comes in to choose some balls. The pictures show the shelves before and after her visit. Which balls did she take away?

Before

After

Lesson 7

CONDITIONAL TENSE (AFFIRMATIVE/NEGATIVE/INTERROGATIVE)

What would you do if you won in the lottery?

Reporter: Paul, what would you do?
Paul: I would buy a big house and a modern car. The remaining money I would invest it in a bank.
Reporter: Very good! And you, Chris?
Chris: Firstly I would pay my debts. Then I would buy a mansion and a big car.
Reporter: Excellent idea!
Reporter: And you, George?
George: I would build a luxurious hotel in front of a beautiful beach in the Northeast of Brazil.
Reporter: What would you do, Sebastian?
Sebastian: I would buy a big farm in Mato Grosso to raise cows and plant soy beans.
Reporter: All of you have good ideas about the use of money. Good luck, but you know: it's very difficult to win money in the lottery.

TEXT COMPREHENSION

1 What would Paul do if he **won** the lottery?
_____

2 What would Chris do if she **won** the lottery?
_____

3 What would George do?
_____

4 What would Sebastian do if he won the lottery?
_____

5 Is it easy to **win** money in the lottery?
_____

LEARN THIS

Conditional tense (Futuro do pretérito).

1. Para se formar o futuro do pretérito, basta colocar o auxiliar **would** antes da forma básica do verbo principal:

   Se você tivesse fome, aonde você iria?

   I would go to a snack bar. (Eu iria a uma lanchonete.)

   Observação:
   Note que não há **s** na terceira pessoa do **conditional tense**:
   Simple present: She eats in a restaurant. (Ela come em um restaurante.)
   Conditional tense: She would eat in a restaurant. (Ela comeria em um restaurante.)

2. Pode-se também usar a forma **should** para as primeiras pessoas (**I, we**):

   We should go by bus. (Nós iríamos de ônibus.)

   A forma auxiliar **should** pode também transmitir o sentido de advertência ou conselho:

   You should drink more water. (Você deveria beber mais água.)

   You should stay home. (Você deveria ficar em casa.)

3. Observe a conjugação do verbo **to like** no **conditional tense**:

Affirmative form	Contracted form
I would like (eu gostaria)	**I'd like**
You would like (você gostaria)	**You'd like**
He would like (ele gostaria)	**He'd like**
She would like (ela gostaria)	**She'd like**
It would like (ele/ela gostaria)	**It'd like**

We would like (nós gostaríamos)   **We'd like**
You would like (vocês gostariam)   **You'd like**
They would like (eles/elas gostariam)   **They'd like**

Interrogative form	Negative form (full form)	(contracted form)
Would I like...?	I would not like	I wouldn't like
Would you like...?	You would not like	You wouldn't like
Would he like...?	He would not like	He wouldn't like
Would she like...?	She would not like	She wouldn't like
Would it like...?	It would not like	It wouldn't like
Would we like...?	We would not like	We wouldn't like
Would you like...?	You would not like	You wouldn't like
Would they like...?	They would not like	They wouldn't like

4. Emprego da conjunção **if**:
   Com a conjunção **if** (se), havendo verbo no presente simples, o outro verbo irá para o futuro do presente:
   If I have money, I will buy a house.   (Se eu tiver dinheiro, comprarei uma casa.)
   If it rains, I will take my umbrella.   (Se chover, levarei meu guarda-chuva.)
   Com a conjunção **if**, havendo verbo no passado, o outro verbo irá para o futuro do pretérito (conditional tense):
   If I had money, I would buy a house.   (Se eu tivesse dinheiro, compraria uma casa.)
   If it rained, I would take my umbrella.   (Se chovesse, levaria meu guarda-chuvas.)

ACTIVITIES

1 Write in the conditional tense:

   a) I – take a taxi   **I would take a taxi.**

   b) He – take a bus   _____

   c) She – eat the cake   _____

   d) They – pay the bill   _____

   e) We – go with you   _____

2 Change to the negative form:

   a) I would buy this book.   **I would not buy this book.**   **I wouldn't buy this book.**

   b) They would pay the bill.

   _____

   _____

c) You would tell the truth.

d) She would talk to him.

3 Follow the pattern. Use the conditional tense:
   a) **She – buy a car – had money**   She would buy a car if she had money.
   b) We – buy a house – had money

   c) They – pay the bill – had money

   d) I – write a letter – had time

   e) They – go to the beach – the weather was good

   f) He – read this book – understood English

4 Follow the pattern. Use **if** and the future tense:
   a) **I – have time – visit you**   If I have time, I will visit you.
   b) You – read this book – learn many things

   c) She – finds the address – write to him

   d) We – go to Italy – send you a postcard

5 Complete with will or would:
   a) I _____ sell this old house, if I had a new one.

   b) If my parents agree, I _____ buy a motorcycle.

c) If it was necessary, I _____ take this medicine.

d) They _____ arrive on time, if they run.

e) If she was my friend, I _____ go to her party.

f) If they are honest men, they _____ pay you.

g) If they were honest men, they _____ pay us.

h) You _____ work, if you are well.

i) We _____ be friends, if you wanted.

j) If he studies, he _____ pass the examination.

FUN TIME

Complete the crossword:
a) Eu venderia: **I would**...
b) Ela escreveria: **She would**...
c) Ele teria: **He would**...
d) Nós tomaríamos um táxi: **We would**... **a taxi**
e) Eles amariam: **They would**...
f) Você pagaria: **You would**...
g) Jane conversaria: **Jane would**...
h) Eu leria: **I would**...
i) Eu contaria: **I would**...
j) Ela ajudaria: **She would**...
k) Nós gostaríamos: **We would**...
l) Eles comeriam: **They would**...

forty-seven **47**

Lesson 8

QUESTION TAGS

At the airport customs

Officer: You have something to declare, don't you?
James: No, I have nothing important to declare.
Officer: This is your suitcase, isn't it?
James: Yes, it is.
Officer: Open it, please.
James: OK.
Officer: These Swiss watches are yours, aren't they?
James: No, they are not mine. One is for my wife and the other is for my son.
Officer: Ok. This perfume is not yours, is it?
James: No, it is for my daughter. She loves French perfume.
Officer: These Italian wine bottles are yours, aren't they?
James: Yes, they are mine. I love Italian wine.
Officer: So do I.
James: Take one bottle for you.
Officer: Thank you, I can't take anything. It's all right. Close your suitcase. You may go.

TEXT COMPREHENSION

1. Where's James?

2. Who examines James' suitcase at the airport?

3. Did James declare important things in his suitcase?

4. Name the things the officer found in James' suitcase.

5. Did the officer find anything important in James´ suitcase?

6. What did James buy for his wife?

7. What's the origin of the perfume?

8. Who loves French perfume?

9. Where are the wine bottles from?

10. Does the officer like Italian wine?

11. James offered a bottle of Italian wine to the officer. Did he accept it?

12. Is the officer an honest man?

LEARN THIS

QUESTION TAG

Question tag é uma interrogação rápida que se faz ao final da frase; é como uma confirmação do que se diz. Se a primeira parte da frase for afirmativa, a segunda parte será negativa e vice-versa.

1. **Question tag** com verbos auxiliares
   This perfume is yours, isn't it?
   Este perfume é seu, não é?
   1ª parte afirmativa – final negativo.
   This perfume isn't yours, is it?
   Este perfume não é seu, é?
   1ª parte negativa – final afirmativo.

2. Quando os verbos não são auxiliares, empregamos as formas verbais:
   a) **do**, **does**, **don't**, **doesn't** para o presente;
   b) **did**, **didn't** para o passado.

Observe outros exemplos:
It is fresh, isn't it?
She was here, wasn't she?
Paul isn't a good boy, is he?
They were friends, weren't they?
Mary has a car, hasn't she?
She can't run, can she?
You can help him, can't you?
They can work, can't they?
They could work, couldn't they?

Exemplos:

You know England, don't you? (Você conhece a Inglaterra, não conhece?)

She doesn't speak English, does she? (Ela não fala Inglês, fala?)

She didn't speak English, did she? (Ela não falou inglês, falou?)

3. **Question tag** com o futuro e o condicional

You will go, won't you? (Você irá, não irá?)

She would come, wouldn't she? (Ele viria, não viria?)

He won't come in time, will he? (Ele não virá a tempo, virá?)

He wouldn't go, would he? (Ele não iria, iria?)

ACTIVITIES

1 Complete with the correct tags:

a) She was in the garden, _____

b) She is alone, _____

c) You are my friend, _____

d) They were busy, _____

e) He can walk, _____

f) It is interesting, _____

g) It is difficult, _____

h) It was necessary, _____

i) Mary can play the guitar, _____

j) Robert could sleep, _____

2 Complete with tags:

a) She isn't a pretty girl, _____

b) They can't run, _____

c) Jane couldn't sleep, _____

d) Peter wasn't busy, _____

e) It isn't difficult, _____

f) You weren't afraid, _____

g) She wasn't tired, _____

h) He can't speak English, _____

i) They aren't careful, _____

j) It isn't a fresh fish, _____

k) She can't drive the car, _____

3 Complete with the correct tags:

a) Mary is very beautiful, _____

b) Jane isn't a teacher, _____

c) It is cold today, _____

d) They aren't friends, _____

e) You were busy, _____

f) You can't walk, _____

g) It was necessary, _____

h) He couldn't sleep, _____

i) You are enemies, _____

j) She can help him, _____

k) They were sure, _____

l) You weren't alone, _____

m) Rose can play the guitar, _____

n) Robert was afraid, _____

4 Complete with tags. Use **don't** or **doesn't**:

a) They like you, _____

b) Alice loves John, _____

c) These girls dance very well, _____

d) You speak English, _____

e) He drives very well, _____

f) Renata wants to marry Charles, _____

g) You know the address, _____

h) She plays the piano, _____

i) The class starts at eight, _____

j) The boys like football, _____

k) He tells the truth, _____

l) Your parents live in Brasília, _____

m) Those men smoke too much, _____

5 Complete with tags. Use **did** or **didn't**:

a) He drove the bus, _____

b) She ate the cake, _____

c) They didn't sleep, _____

d) You didn't see him, _____

e) Mary told a lie, _____

f) They lived in London for a long time, _____
_____

g) He woke early in the morning, _____
_____

h) Robert didn't buy a car, _____

6 Complete with tags. Use **will** or **won't**:

a) Ruth will go next week, _____

b) Paul won't come next month, _____

c) Joseph will come tomorrow, _____

d) She will give him a present, _____

e) Louis will give you some information,
_____

f) Barbara and Helen won't travel, _____

g) Alfred and Douglas will travel next month, _____

7 Complete with tags. Use **would** or **wouldn't**:

a) You wouldn't sell you car, _____

b) They would tell the truth, _____

c) She would travel to Europe, _____

d) He wouldn't help you, _____

fifty-one 51

Lesson 9
COMPARATIVE OF EQUALITY, SUPERIORITY AND INFERIORITY

Which is more beautiful?
Which of these cars is more beautiful?
The old car or the modern one?

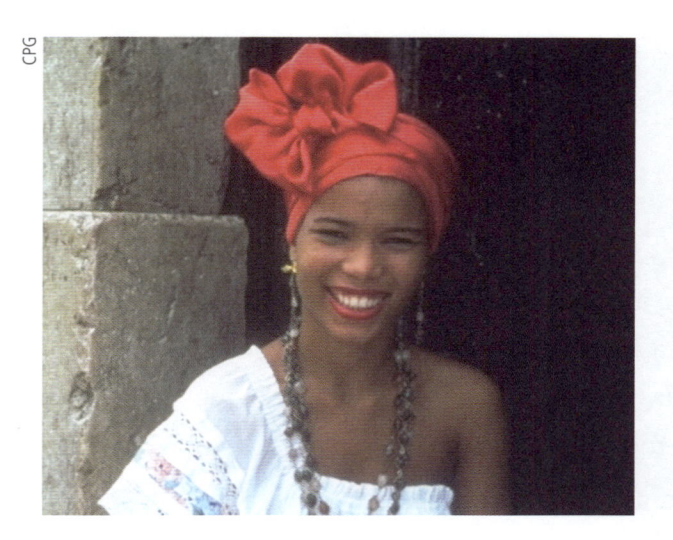

Brazilian girls are pretty. American girls are pretty, too.
Brazilian girls are as pretty as American girls.

Winter is a cold season. Summer is a hot season.
Winter is colder than summer. Summer is hotter than winter.

A Mercedes-Benz is expensive. A Ferrari is very expensive.
A Ferrari is more expensive than a Mercedes-Benz.

LEARN THIS

COMPARATIVE DEGREE OF THE ADJECTIVES

Grau comparativo dos adjetivos

1. Com adjetivos curtos (1 ou 2 sílabas)
   - Comparativo de igualdade (**equality**): ... **as** + **adjective** + **as**...
     Monica is as pretty as Roberta. (Monica é tão bonita quanto Roberta.)
   - Comparativo de superioridade (**superiority**): ... **adjective** + **er** + **than** (do que) ...
     Winter is colder than summer. (O inverno é mais frio do que o verão.)

2. Com adjetivos longos (2 ou mais sílabas): ... **as** + **adjective** + **as**...
   - Comparativo de igualdade (**equality**)
     Carol is as beautiful as Jane. (Carol é tão bonita quanto Jane.)
   - Comparativo de superioridade (**superiority**): ... **more** + **adjective** + **than** ...
     Your house is more comfortable than mine. (Sua casa é mais confortável do que a minha.)

3. Comparativo de inferioridade (**inferiority**): ... **less** + **adjective** + **than** ...
   - **This lesson is less difficult than the first one**. (Esta lição é menos difícil do que a primeira.)
     (A expressão **less... than** é pouco usada.)
   - **This lesson is not so difficult as the first one**. (Esta lição não é tão difícil quanto a primeira.)
     (A expressão **not so... as** é mais usada.)

Observações

1. Alguns adjetivos curtos terminados por vogal + consoante dobram a consoante no comparativo de superioridade:
   big ⇒ **bigger than**
   hot ⇒ **hotter than**
   fat ⇒ **fatter than**
   thin ⇒ **thinner than**

2. Quando o adjetivo termina por **y** precedido de consoante, substituímos o **y** por **ier** no comparativo de superioridade:
   dirty ⇒ **dirtier than**
   pretty ⇒ **prettier than**
   happy ⇒ **happier than**
   easy ⇒ **easier than**

3. Alguns adjetivos têm comparativo irregular:
   good ⇒ **better than** (melhor do que)
   bad ⇒ **worse than** (pior do que)

ACTIVITIES

1 Write the sentences in the comparative of equality:

a) I – strong – you
   I am as strong as you.

b) She – beautiful – you

c) My house – comfortable – yours

d) Today – cold – yesterday

e) My school – good – yours

f) The train – fast – the bus

2 Use the comparative of superiority:

a) Mr. Goldman – rich – Mr. Pauper
   Mr. Goldman is richer than Mr. Pauper.

b) My pencil – long – yours

c) I – strong – you

d) Paul – old – Mary

e) Mary – young – Paul

f) My course – easy – yours

g) Your city – dirty – mine

h) Lucy – pretty – Monica

i) Gordon – fat – Mr Finn

j) Today – hot – yesterday

k) My country – big – yours

l) Your house – comfortable – mine

m) A Mercedes-Benz – expensive – a Gol

n) Mathematics – difficult – Portuguese

o) Rio de Janeiro – beautiful – my city

3 Use the comparative of inferiority:

a) Bob – rich – James   **Bob is not so rich as James.   Bob is less rich than James.**

b) Lucy – beautiful – her sister

c) Today – cold – yesterday

d) Bill – fat – Jordan

e) Portuguese – difficult – Japanese

REVIEW

1 Complete the sentences using the correct tags:

a) She was alone, _____

b) It is difficult, _____

c) You are right, _____

d) She can walk, _____

e) It wasn't necessary, _____

f) They couldn't go, _____

g) She isn't well, _____

h) You aren't at home, _____

i) You speak English, _____

j) They know the address, _____

k) She plays the piano, _____

l) John knows you, _____

2 Complete the sentences using the conditional tense:

a) **If I had money... (buy a car)**
   If I had money I would buy a car.

b) If I had money... (buy a motorcycle)
   _____

c) If I had time... (write a letter)
   _____

3 Complete the sentences using the future tense:

a) **If the weather is good... (go to the beach)**
   If the weather is good I will go to the beach.

b) If you run... (arrive on time)
   _____

c) If they are honest... (pay the bill)
   _____

4 Use the comparative of superiority:

a) **This lesson – easy – the first one**
   This lesson is easier than the first on.

b) Peter – fat – Fred
   _____

c) Today – hot – yesterday
   _____

d) Your city – big – mine
   _____

e) Japanese – difficult – English
   _____

5 Use the comparative of inferiority:

a) **George – rich – Paul**   **George is not so rich as Paul.**   **George is less rich than Paul.**

b) Today – hot – yesterday

c) English – difficult – French

_____

_____

_____

_____

FUN TIME

Changing letters

1 If you change one letter of the words below, you will have the correct answers.

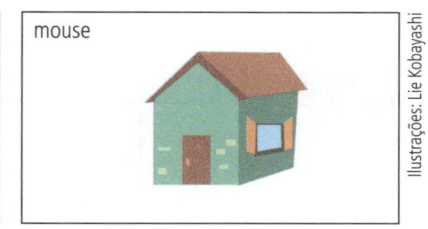

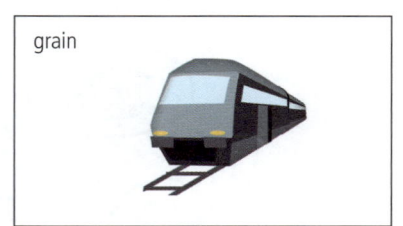

look	lake	mouse
dish	short	grain

2 Why did the boy throw the butter out of the window?

_____

_____

fifty-seven **57**

3 Complete the crossword according to the pictures:

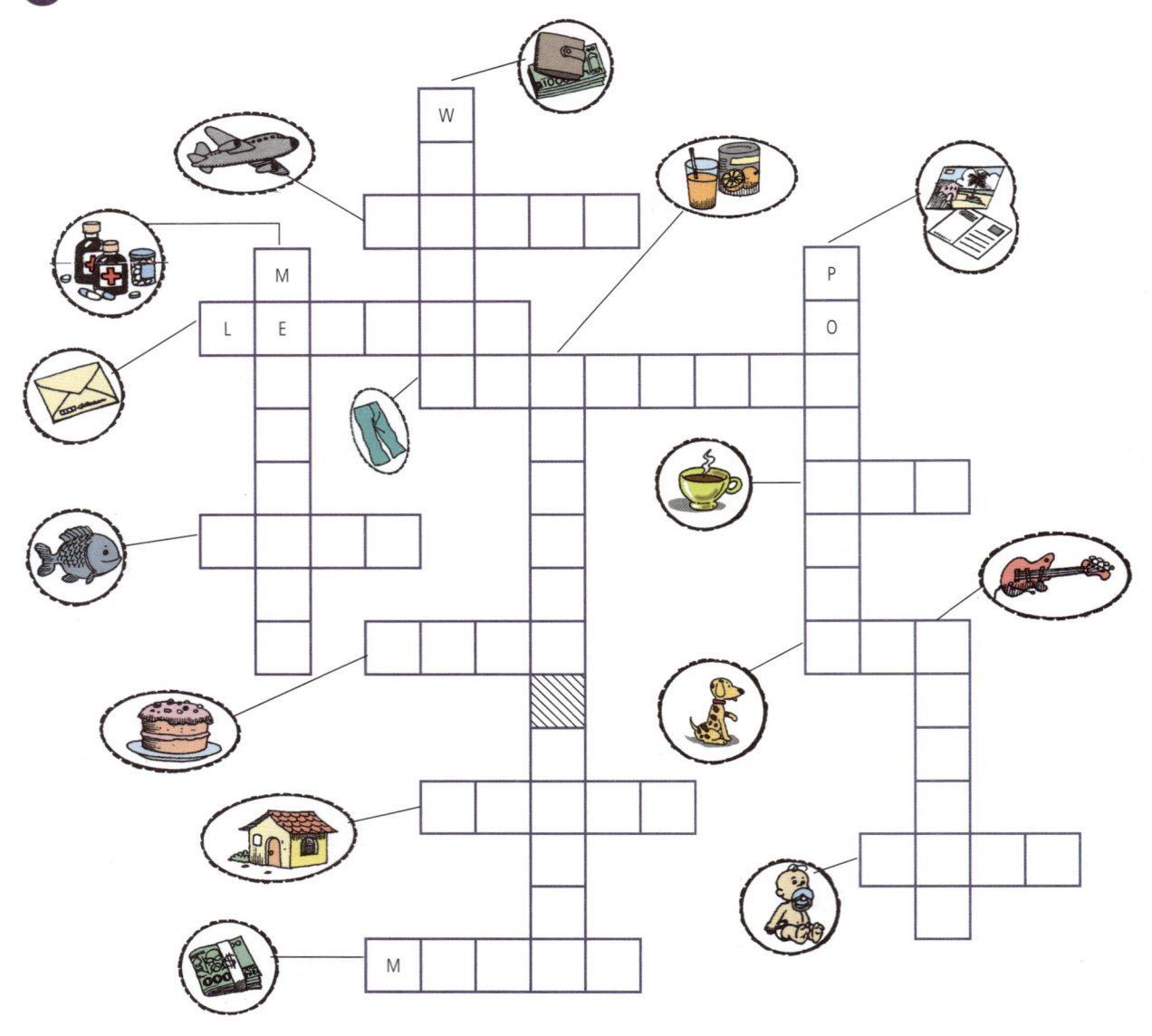

Lesson 10

SUPERLATIVE DEGREE OF ADJECTIVES

The Burj Al Arab

The most luxurious hotel in the world

The Burj Al Arab is the world's unique 7 star hotel.
This hotel rests on an artificial island constructed 280 meters from the beach in Dubai in the Persian Gulf. It has 202 bedroom suites. Its atrium is 180 meters high.
The smallest suite occupies 169 square meters and the largest 780 square meters.
The cost of staying in a suite begins at 1.000 dollars to 28.000 dollars per night.
This hotel has a shape of a sail ship.

Iguaçu Falls

The most wonderful waterfalls in the world

These waterfalls are located on the border of the Brazilian state of Paraná and the Argentine province of Missiones.

Its name comes from the Tupi Guarani language: Igu (y) = water + açu = big →
→ Iguaçu = big water

The Iguaçu waterfalls consist of 275 falls along 2.7 kilometers of the Iguaçu river. Some of the falls are up to 80 meters high but the majority are about 65 meters high. The most famous fall is the Devil's Throat.

When Eleonor Roosevelt (the president's wife of the United States) visited the Iguaçu Falls she was astonished at the extreme beauty of the falls and exclaimed: "Poor Niagara!" comparing our falls with the Niagara Falls in the United States.

TEXT COMPREHENSION

Text A

1. Where is the most luxurious hotel in the world?

___

2. Is the Burj Al Arab hotel in the continent?

___

60 sixty

3 How many bedroom suites does the Burj Al Arab have?
_____

4 How many square meters does the largest suite have?
_____

5 What is the shape of the hotel?
_____

Text B

1 Where are located the most wonderful waterfalls in the world?
_____

2 What's the origin of the word Iguaçu?
_____

3 How many falls does the Iguaçu Falls have?
_____

4 What is the height of the falls?
_____

5 What is the name of the most famous fall in Iguaçu Falls?
_____

6 According to Eleonor Roosevelt, are the Niagara Falls more beautiful than Iguaçu Falls?
_____

LEARN THIS

Superlative degree

O superlativo, em inglês, é formado de duas maneiras:

1ª Com adjetivos curtos (até duas sílabas)
   Acrescenta-se **est** ao adjetivo:
   - **rich**: **the richest**
     Paul is the richest man in the city. (Paul é o homem mais rico da cidade.)
   - **tall**: **the tallest**
     John is the tallest boy in my class. (John é o menino mais alto da minha classe.)
   - **heavy**: **the heaviest**
     Gordon is the heaviest in my team. (Gordon é o mais pesado do meu time.)
   - **easy**: **the easiest**
     It is the easiest lesson in my book. (É a lição mais fácil do meu livro.)

2ª Com adjetivos longos (duas ou mais sílabas)
Antepõe-se a expressão **the most** ao adjetivo, que fica invariável:
- **important**: **the most important**
  He is the most important man in the firm. (Ele é o homem mais importante da firma.)
- **beautiful**: **the most beautiful**
  She is the most beautiful girl in my class. (Ela é a garota mais linda da minha classe.)
- **common**: **the most common**
  It is the most common fact in our days. (É o fato mais comum em nossos dias.)

Observações

Observação: alguns adjetivos têm o superlativo irregular:
good (bom); **the best** (o melhor)
bad (mau); **the worst** (o pior)

ACTIVITIES

1) Write the sentences in the superlative degree. Follow the pattern:

a) **Everest – high peak – in the world**
   The Everest is the highest peak in the world.
   (It is located in Nepal, a country just in the north of India. It measures 8,848 meters.)

b) Sahara – large desert – in – the world
   _____

c) The elephant – one of – great animals on Earth
   _____

d) The whale – heavy and big animal – in the sea
   (It can measure 33 meters and weigh about 120 tons.)
   _____

e) Rio-Niterói – long bridge – in Brazil
   _____

2) Write in the superlative degree:

a) **This lesson – easy – in the book**
   This lesson is the easiest in the book.

b) This class – dirty – in the school
   _____

c) John – lazy boy – in my class
   _____

d) This – dry region – in Brazil
   _____

3 Write the sentences using the superlative degree:

a) Paul – strong – in my class
   Paul is the strongest in my class.

b) Today – cold day – in the month
   _____

c) Gordon – clever boy – in my team
   _____

4 Write the sentences in the superlative degree. Use **the most**:

a) He – important man – in the firm
   _____

b) She – beautiful girl – at the party
   _____

c) It – comfortable car – in our factory
   _____

d) This – interesting book – in the library
   _____

e) São Paulo – populous city – in Brazil
   _____

f) Rio de Janeiro – marvelous city – in Brazil
   _____

LET'S SING

My love

My love is warmer than the warmest sunshine,
Softer than a sigh.
My love is deeper than the deepest ocean,
Wider than the sky.
My love is brighter than the brightest star
That shines every night above,
And there is nothing in this world
That can ever change my love.
(An American folk song)

Word bank

warm: quente
deep: profundo
sunshine: brilho do sol
wide: amplo, largo
soft: suave
bright: brilhante
sigh: suspiro
shine: brilhar

Antes de cantar a música, ouça o professor ou o CD, prestando atenção na pronúncia das palavras. Procure, também, saber o significado delas.

Lesson 11

PRESENT PERFECT TENSE

Technology

In our days man has reached fabulous progress in Science and Technology.

He has built modern bridges, dams, power stations and has dominated some forces of nature.

He has invented many types of machines to improve his life on Earth. Among these inventions we can mention: television, telephone, computers, refrigerators, cameras, means of transportation and so on.

Man has sent spaceships to other planets and little by little he is concquering the universe.

Man has already controlled some bad diseases by means of the modern resources of medicine.

But there are so many things to do in the future!

For example:
- Man hasn't found the cure for cancer yet.
- Man hasn't put an end to war.
- Man hasn't solved the problem of hunger and many other social problems.
- Man hasn't learnt how to protect nature from pollution and destruction yet.

TEXT COMPREHENSION

1 In which fields has man made fabulous progress?
_____

2 Can you mention some man's inventions?
_____

3 Has man reached other planets?
_____

4 Which of these has man already reached?
 ( ) Venus
 ( ) Moon
 ( ) Uranus

5 Has man already controlled all bad diseases?
_____

6 Can you mention a bad disease that man hasn't controlled yet?
_____

7 Which are some of the great problems that man has to solve in the future?
_____

LEARN THIS

Man has built modern bridges. (O homem tem construído pontes modernas.)
O **present perfect tense** consiste no emprego do verbo **to have** (ter) no presente do indicativo seguido do particípio passado do verbo principal:

has
have + past participle

sixty-five **65**

Present perfect tense

O **present perfect tense** deve ser usado nos seguintes casos:

1. Quando relatamos uma ação ocorrida no tempo passado, mas sem que determinemos a data ou o momento em que ela ocorreu ou foi realizada.

   I have slept late. (Eu tenho dormido tarde.)

   He has got up early. (Ele tem levantado cedo.)

   Se determinarmos a data ou o momento em que a ação se realiza, porém, devemos empregar o **simple past tense**:

   I slept late yesterday. (Eu dormi tarde ontem.)

   He got up early last Sunday. (Ele levantou cedo no último domingo.)

2. Quando nos referimos a uma ação (ou fato) que começou no passado mas que ainda persiste até o momento presente.

   I have worked here since 1990. (Eu trabalho aqui desde 1990.)

   He has lived in Brazil for ten months. (Ele mora no Brasil há dez meses.)

3. Quando nos referimos a uma ação (ou fato) que se repete várias vezes no passado, sem menção do tempo exato.

   I have visited my parents many times. (Eu tenho visitado meus pais várias vezes)

4. Quando nos referimos a uma ação que acabou de ser feita.

   He has just arrived. (Ele acabou de chegar.)

   I have just send the letter. (Acabei de enviar a carta.)

Observações

O **present perfect tense** é frequentemente acompanhado de algumas preposições ou advérbios. Observe:

Just: **She has just arrived**.
(Ela acabou de chegar.)

Ever: **Have you ever been to England?**
(Você já esteve na Inglaterra?)

Never: **No, I've never been to England**.
(Não, eu nunca estive na Inglaterra.)

Already: **They have already arrived**.
(Eles já chegaram.)

Yet: **No, they haven't arrived yet**.
(Não, eles não chegaram ainda.)

Since: **I haven't seen Mr Jones since Sunday**.
(Eu não vejo o Sr. Jones desde domingo.)

For: **We have lived here for 10 years**.
(Nós moramos aqui por 10 anos.)

ACTIVITIES

1 Fill in the blanks with the correct form of underlined verb:

**a) I work here now. (Simple Present)
I have worked here for a month. (Present Perfect)**

b) I live in São Paulo.

   I have _____ in São Paulo for five years.

c) They go out on Sundays.

   They have _____ several times this year.

d) I study in the morning.

   I have _____ during two mornings this week.

e) Joseph plays the piano very well.

   He has _____ in several recitals.

f) Jane cooks very well.

   She has _____ many delicious meals for me.

g) Bob reads a lot.

   He has _____ many books this year.

h) Mr Jones loves to tell stories.

   He has _____ us some funny ones.

i) Our maid breaks things all the time.

   She has _____ many glasses this month.

j) The secretary writes many letters.

   She has _____ many letters this year.

k) I often visit my relatives.

   I have _____ them many times this year.

2 Choose the correct verb form:

a) I went out yesterday.

   ( ) went out   ( ) have gone out

b) A thief _____ Mr Black's watch last night.
   ( ) has stolen   ( ) stole

c) I _____ you for a month.
   ( ) didn't see   ( ) haven't seen

d) He is a good barber. He _____ my hair for years.
   ( ) cut   ( ) has cut

sixty-seven **67**

e) Jane _____ English for many years.
   ( ) taught   ( ) has taught

f) He _____ something for his house last week.
   ( ) bought   ( ) has bought

g) They _____ yet.
   ( ) didn't come   ( ) haven't come

h) I _____ never _____ in a bank.
   ( ) didn't work   ( ) have...worked

i) _____ you already _____ that film?
   ( ) Did... see   ( ) Have... seen

j) No, I _____ it yet.
   ( ) haven't seen ( ) didn't see

k) I _____ my watch last week.
   ( ) have broken   ( ) broke

l) I _____ Mary last night.
   ( ) saw   ( ) have seen

m) I _____ for Rio last night.
   ( ) left   ( ) have left

n) She _____ just _____ the door.
   ( ) opened   ( ) has...opened

3 Complete the sentences with the correct form of the verb:

a) (pay) Have you _____ all the bills?

b) (find) She hasn't _____ the keys yet.

c) (speak) The teacher hasn't _____ to me yet.

d) (receive) I haven't _____ any mail since Sunday.

e) (send) He hasn't _____ any books yet.

f) (make) I haven't _____ any mistakes yet.

g) (read) I haven't _____ any books recently.

Observações

Usa-se **yet** em frases interrogativas e negativas. **Yet** vem sempre no final da sentença.
Have you made the beds yet? (Você não arrumou as camas ainda?)
No, I haven't made the beds yet. (Não, eu ainda não arrumei as camas.)
Already é usado em frases afirmativas e também em interrogativas:
Have they already eaten? (Eles já comeram?)
Yes, they have already eaten. (Sim, eles já comeram.)
A posição de **already** vem antes do particípio passado do verbo.

68 sixty-eight

4 Change to the negative form. Follow the pattern.
   a) Mary has already found her keys.
   Mary hasn't found her keys yet.
   b) They have already eaten.
   _____

   c) She has already woken up.
   _____

   d) I have already seen that film.
   _____

   e) John has already bought the car.
   _____

   f) She has already made the beds.
   _____

   g) I have already visited Rio.
   _____

5 Fill in the blanks with the present perfect tense of the verbs in parenthesis.
   a) (speak) I have spoken to him about this several times.
   b) (see) I _____ that film several times.
   c) (lend) I _____ money to my friend.
   d) (learn) We _____ many new words in this course.
   e) (make) She _____ the same mistakes.
   f) (be) I _____ never _____ to England.
   g) (hear) I _____ this story several times.
   h) (travel) They _____ all over the world.
   i) (live) We _____ in São Paulo since 1980.
   j) (work) John _____ very hard recently.
   k) (teach) He _____ English for many years.
   l) (rain) It _____ all day long.
   m) (be) She _____ sick for three days.
   n) (live) I _____ in this house since my childhood.
   o) (rain) It hasn't _____ since May.
   p) (eat) They haven't _____ yet.
   q) (leave) They haven't _____ yet.
   r) (wake up) She hasn't _____ yet.
   s) (go) They haven't _____ to the beach yet.
   t) (shut) I have already _____ the doors.
   u) (make) She has already _____ the beds.
   v) (catch) I have already _____ two fish.
   w) (buy) I have already _____ the vegetables.

FUN TIME

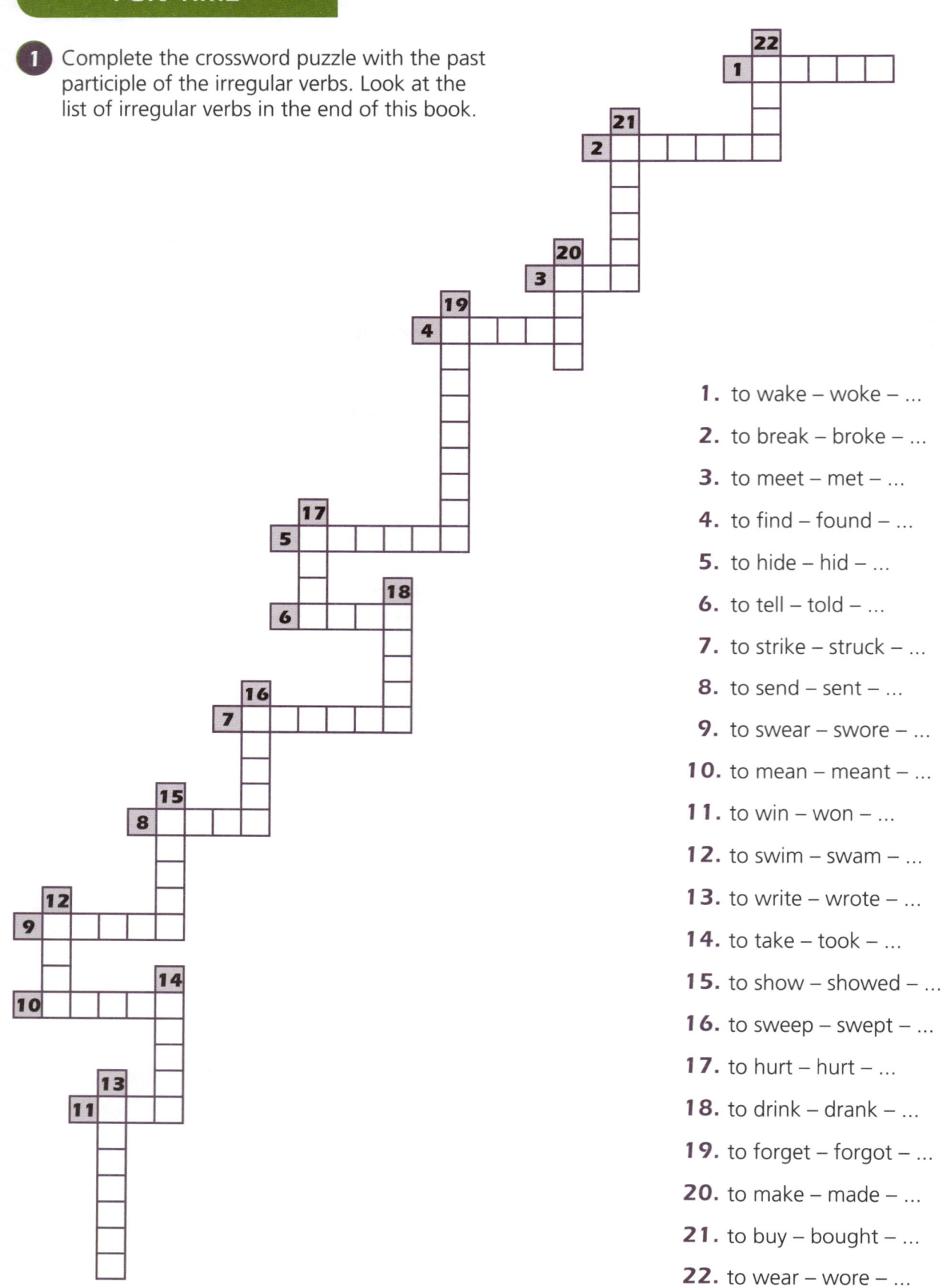

1 Complete the crossword puzzle with the past participle of the irregular verbs. Look at the list of irregular verbs in the end of this book.

1. to wake – woke – ...
2. to break – broke – ...
3. to meet – met – ...
4. to find – found – ...
5. to hide – hid – ...
6. to tell – told – ...
7. to strike – struck – ...
8. to send – sent – ...
9. to swear – swore – ...
10. to mean – meant – ...
11. to win – won – ...
12. to swim – swam – ...
13. to write – wrote – ...
14. to take – took – ...
15. to show – showed – ...
16. to sweep – swept – ...
17. to hurt – hurt – ...
18. to drink – drank – ...
19. to forget – forgot – ...
20. to make – made – ...
21. to buy – bought – ...
22. to wear – wore – ...

70 seventy

Lesson 12
ACTIVE VOICE AND PASSIVE VOICE

The first Americans

Robert: Do you know who were the first Americans?
Liz: The first Americans were the Indians.
Robert: How did the American Indians live?
Liz: They lived in groups called tribes.
Robert: Were all the tribes the same?
Liz: No, the tribes had different names and different ways of life.
Robert: Can you tell me some names of American Indian tribes?
Liz: Yes, here are some of them: Cherokee, Cheyenne, Chinook, Navajo, Sioux, Blackfoot, Redskin, Nez Percé, Apache, etc.
Robert: Can you tell me something about one of these tribes?
Liz: Yes. The Sioux, for example, lived on the plains. They were hunters. Their houses were covered by buffalo skins. They ate buffalo meat and used its skin as clothing.
Robert: And what about the Hopi tribe?
Liz: The Hopi tribe lived in the desert of Arizona. Their houses were built with rock and mud. Their clothing was made of sheep wool.

TEXT COMPREHENSION

1 Who were the first Americans?
_____

2 The American Indians lived:
( ) alone ( ) in groups

3 A group of Indians who live together is called
( ) an Indian community ( ) a village ( ) a tribe

4 Are all the Indian tribes the same?
_____

5 Can you mention the names of some American Indian tribes?
_____

6 Where did the Sioux live?
_____

7 The Sioux Indians were:
( ) fishermen ( ) hunters

8 The Sioux's homes were covered:
( ) by tiles ( ) by buffalo's skin

9 What did the Sioux eat?
_____

10 What did the Sioux wear as clothing?
_____

11 Where did the Hopi tribe live?
_____

12 The Hopi´s houses were built with:
( ) brick and mortar (mortar: cement, sand and lime)
( ) rock and mud
( ) wood

13 The Hopi's clothing was made of:
( ) cotton ( ) linen ( ) wool

LEARN THIS

Há duas formas estruturais de verbos:

a) Active voice (voz ativa)

Na voz ativa a ênfase está em quem pratica a ação. É a voz que usamos normalmente.

ACTIVE VOICE		
sujeito	verbo	objeto
The baby	drinks	milk
The dogs	eat	meat

b) Passive voice (voz passiva)

Na voz passiva a ênfase está na ação praticada. É menos usual, mas, às vezes, necessitamos usar essa estrutura.

c) A voz passiva consiste no emprego do verbo **to be** mais o particípio passado do verbo principal.

PASSIVE VOICE		
sujeito	verbo	objeto
Milk	is drunk	by the baby
Meat	is eaten	by the dogs

Observações

d) O particípio passado (**past participle**) dos verbos regulares tem a mesma forma que o **past tense**, termina em **ed**.

REGULAR VERBS		
Infinitive	Past tense	Past participle
to live	lived	**lived** = morado
to cover	covered	**covered** = coberto
to use	used	**used** = usado

e) Os verbos irregulares (**irregular verbs**) possuem terminações muito variadas, por isso é necessário aprendê-los. Veja alguns exemplos:

IRREGULAR VERBS		
Infinitive	Past tense	Past participle
to know	knew	**known** = conhecido
to have	had	**had** = tido
To make	made	**made** = feito

A estrutura da voz passiva é simples:

Sujeito + verbo auxiliar (**be**) + verbo principal no **past participle** + **by** + agente da passiva

Sujeito +	verbo auxiliar (be) +	verbo principal no past participle +	by +	agente da passiva
Coffee	is	made	by	the maid

Observações: O agente da passiva só é mencionado quando necessário.

O verbo auxiliar (**be**) é conjugado no mesmo tempo verbal que se pretende apresentar a ação praticada. Deve também concordar com o sujeito. Veja alguns exemplos de como transformar sentenças na voz ativa (**active voice**) para voz passiva (**passive voice**).

Active voice: **The teacher corrects the exercises.** (present)
Passive voice: **The exercises are corrected by the teacher.**
Active voice: **The boy used the computer.** (past)
Passive voice: **The computer was used by the boy.**
Active voice: **The students will answer the questions.** (future)
Passive voice: **The questions will be answered by the students.**

ACTIVITIES

1 Change the sentences to the passive voice (verbs in the present tense):

a) **Jane invites Sara.**
   Sara is invited by Jane.

b) The boys receive a message.

c) A child opens the door.

d) Monica invites George to the party.

e) The teacher corrects the exercise.

f) The pupils answer all the questions.

2 Change the sentences to the passive voice (verbs in the past tense)

a) **An Indian receives a message.**
   A message was received by an Indian.

b) A child opened the door.

c) She cleaned the room.

d) Trucks transported heavy goods.

e) The postman delivered the letters.

f) The doctors examined the patients carefully.

g) The maids washed the windows.

3 Change the sentences to the passive voice (verbs in the future tense)

a) Indians will cover the houses with buffalo skins.
The houses will be covered with buffalo skins by the Indians.

b) The teacher will explain the lesson.
_____

c) The teacher will punish the lazy boys.
_____

d) She will invite you to the party.
_____

e) The students will correct the exercises.
_____

f) The postman will deliver the letters.
_____

g) The goalkeeper will pass the ball.
_____

IRREGULAR VERBS		
to build	built	built
to buy	bought	bought
to see	saw	seen
to catch	caught	caught
to sell	sold	sold

4 Change the sentences to the passive voice (irregular verbs)

a) The Indians built houses.
Houses were built by the Indians.

b) They will pay the bill.
_____

c) He bought a red car.
_____

d) We saw the documents.
_____

e) The police will catch the thief.
_____

f) John will sell the house next year.
_____

REVIEW

1 Write the sentences using the superlative:

a) The Rolls-Royce – expensive car in the world
The Rolls-Royce is the most expensive car in the world.

b) He – old man in the world
_____

c) He – tall man in the world
_____

seventy-five **75**

d) The Everest – high peak in the world
___

e) The Sahara – large desert in the world
___

f) Angel Falls – high waterfall in the world
___

g) The elephant – heavy animal on Earth
___

h) The whale – big animal that lives in water
___

i) Miriam – pretty girl in my class
___

j) Rio-Niterói – long bridge in Brazil
___

k) He – happy man in the world
___

l) Winter – the cold season of the year
___

2 Change to the passive voice:

a) **Monica invited John.**
John was invited by Monica.

b) Graham Bell invented the telephone.
___

c) Mary wrote a letter.
___

d) Trucks transport heavy loads.
___

e) The gardener plants flowers.
___

3 Complete the sentences using the present perfect tense:

a) (work)   I _____ here for many years.

b) (live)   She _____ in São Paulo for ten years.

c) (visited) I _____ my relatives.

d) (write)   The secretary _____ many letters.

e) (arrive)   She _____ just _____.

4 Choose the correct alternative – simple past or present perfect tense:

a) I _____ a present for you yesterday.
   ( ) have bought   ( ) bought

b) I _____ never _____ in a bank.
   ( ) don't... work   ( ) have... worked

c) _____ you already _____ that film?
   ( ) Did... see   ( ) Have... seen

d) I _____ the teacher last night.
   ( ) have seen   ( ) saw

e) A thief _____ my wallet yesterday.
   ( ) has stolen   ( ) stole

FUN TIME

What's the easiest way to double your money?
_____

— I have already read the first page.
  Can you turn it?

No words

Lesson 13

INDEFINITE ADJECTIVES AND PRONOUNS

Education

The word education has several meanings. Anything that you learn in life is considered part of your education. You can learn from television, radio, books, magazines, newspapers, the daily observation of things and contact with other people.

Formal Education
Formal education is the education (that) you get in school.
Informal Education
Informal education is the education (that) you get outside school.
What is the aim of education?
Here are some different ideas about the aim of education:
- One of the purposes of education is to preserve the great things of the past.
- By means of education you get good manners to live in society.
- Education is to learn facts.
- Education makes a person inquire about facts.
- Education helps a person to grow and learn all that is necessary in life.
- The main purpose of education is to give the student the understanding of the world he lives in and help him to solve his own problems.
- Children learn more rapidly when they do the things that they are learning.

TEXT COMPREHENSION

1 What is the meaning of the word education?
_____

2 Complete: "You can learn from television, _____
_____ people and the daily observation of things."

3 What is formal education?
_____

4 What is informal education?
_____

5 According to you, what is the aim of Education? (Choose one or two aims from the reading.)
_____

6 Complete: "Children learn more rapidly when
_____

LEARN THIS
Indefinites
Look at the examples:

a)

Affirmative form	Negative form
–There are some boys in the class. →	–Há alguns meninos na classe.
–There is some water in the glass. →	–Há alguma água no copo.
–There is somebody in the car. →	–Há alguém no carro.
–There is someone in the car. →	–Há alguém no carro.
–There is something in the box. →	–Há alguma coisa na caixa.

b)

Interrogative form	Negative form
–Is there any water in the glass? →	–No, there isn't any.
–Há alguma água no copo? →	–(Não, não há nenhuma.)
–Is there anybody in the house? →	–No, there isn't anybody.
–Há alguém na casa? →	–(Não, não há ninguém.)
–Is there anything in the box? →	–No, there isn't anything.
–Há alguma coisa na caixa? →	–(Não, não há nada.)

seventy-nine **79**

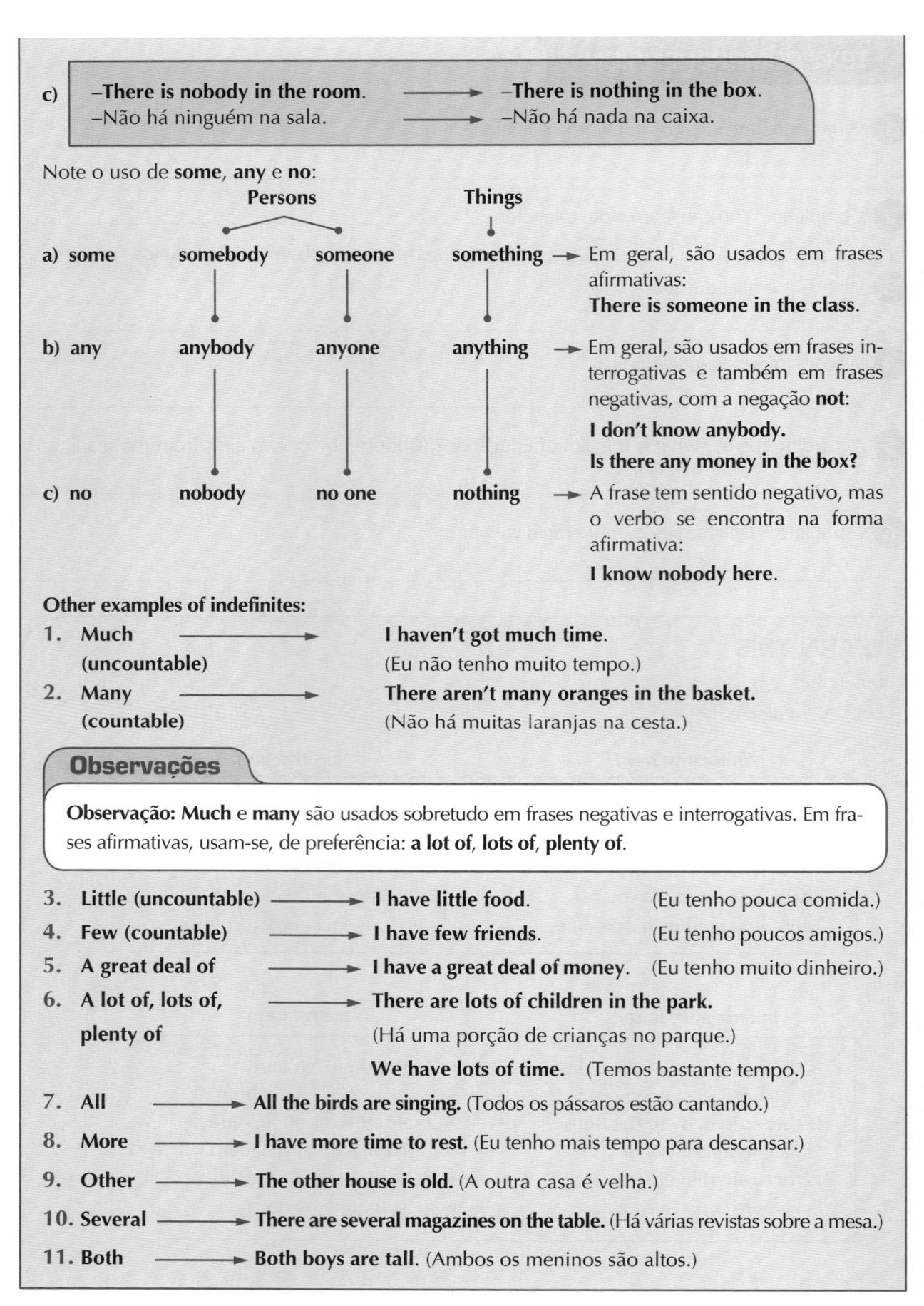

c) –There is nobody in the room. ⟶ –There is nothing in the box.
–Não há ninguém na sala. ⟶ –Não há nada na caixa.

Note o uso de **some**, **any** e **no**:

	Persons		Things	
a) some	somebody	someone	something	⟶ Em geral, são usados em frases afirmativas: **There is someone in the class**.
b) any	anybody	anyone	anything	⟶ Em geral, são usados em frases interrogativas e também em frases negativas, com a negação **not**: **I don't know anybody.** **Is there any money in the box?**
c) no	nobody	no one	nothing	⟶ A frase tem sentido negativo, mas o verbo se encontra na forma afirmativa: **I know nobody here**.

Other examples of indefinites:

1. **Much** ⟶ **I haven't got much time**.
   (uncountable)   (Eu não tenho muito tempo.)
2. **Many** ⟶ **There aren't many oranges in the basket.**
   (countable)   (Não há muitas laranjas na cesta.)

Observações

Observação: Much e **many** são usados sobretudo em frases negativas e interrogativas. Em frases afirmativas, usam-se, de preferência: **a lot of**, **lots of**, **plenty of**.

3. **Little** (uncountable) ⟶ **I have little food.** (Eu tenho pouca comida.)
4. **Few** (countable) ⟶ **I have few friends**. (Eu tenho poucos amigos.)
5. **A great deal of** ⟶ **I have a great deal of money**. (Eu tenho muito dinheiro.)
6. **A lot of, lots of, plenty of** ⟶ **There are lots of children in the park.**
   (Há uma porção de crianças no parque.)
   We have lots of time. (Temos bastante tempo.)
7. **All** ⟶ **All the birds are singing.** (Todos os pássaros estão cantando.)
8. **More** ⟶ **I have more time to rest.** (Eu tenho mais tempo para descansar.)
9. **Other** ⟶ **The other house is old.** (A outra casa é velha.)
10. **Several** ⟶ **There are several magazines on the table.** (Há várias revistas sobre a mesa.)
11. **Both** ⟶ **Both boys are tall**. (Ambos os meninos são altos.)

ACTIVITIES

> **Remember:**
> Usually use   some   in affirmative sentences
>   any   in negative and
>   interrogative sentences

1 Fill in the blanks with some or any.

a) I have _____ friends in Rio.

b) I don´t have _____ money.

c) We made _____ suggestions.

d) The teacher explained _____ problems.

e) I'm learning _____ new words in English.

f) There are _____ people waiting for you.

g) Did you have _____ friends in the United States?

h) The pupils didn't ask _____ questions.

i) There wasn't _____ news.

2 Fill in the blanks with somebody, something, anybody, anything.

a) Helen didn't invite _____ to her birthday party.

b) I want to buy _____ for my friend.

c) Did _____ knock at the door?

d) Is there _____ in the box?

e) No, there isn't _____ in the box.

f) Did you see _____ talking in class?

g) No, I didn't see _____ talking in class.

h) Is there _____ interesting in this paper?

i) No, there isn't _____ interesting in this paper.

> **Remember:**
> Usually use   somebody / someone / something   in affirmative sentences
> Use   anybody / anyone / anything   in negative and interrogative sentences

3 Answer the questions using the pronouns nobody or nothing:

a) Is there anybody in the room?

   No, there is nobody.

b) Is there anything in the box?
   _____

c) Did you buy anything in the supermarket?
   _____

d) Is there anything I can do for you?
   _____

e) Did anybody telephone me?
   _____

f) Did she give anything to you?
   _____

4 Answer the questions affirmatively and negatively.

a) Have you got any coffee? Yes, I have got some. / No, I haven't got any.

b) Have you got any sugar?   _____

c) Have you got any butter?   _____

d) Have you got any money?   _____

e) Has she got any work to do?   _____

f) Have you got any cigarettes?   _____

5 Follow the pattern:

a) I saw something in the box.

   I didn't see anything in the box.

   I saw nothing in the box.

b) I saw somebody in the house.
   _____
   _____

c) I bought something for you.
   _____
   _____

d) I got something interesting.
   _____
   _____

6 Change to the negative form:

a) There are some boys in the class.
   There are not any boys in the class.
   There are no boys in the class.

b) She gave something to me.
She didn't give anything to me.
She gave nothing to me.

c) There is some milk in the glass.

d) There is something to drink.

e) There is someone in the room.

7 Change to the interrogative form:
a) **There are some boys in the park.**
   Are there any boys in the park?
b) **There is somebody in the car.**
   Is there anybody in the car?
c) **You saw somebody in the bank.**
   Did you see anybody in the bank?
d) There are some books on the table.

e) There is something to eat.

f) You received some letters from your friends.

eighty-three **83**

Lesson 14
ADVERBS OF TIME, FREQUENCY, MANNER, PLACE, INTENSITY, NEGATION AND AFFIRMATION

Proverbs

Proverbs are a traditional form of folklore. They are full of wisdom and are frequently used by old people to educate the young.

Proverbs are found everywhere among many peoples in the world.

A proverb can be long or short, in verse or in prose.

Here you have some proverbs; try to understand them and choose those you like most.

Forced love does not last.
Time is money.
A good beginning makes a good ending.
Out of sight, out of mind.
Love is blind.
Two heads are better than one.
All is well when ends well.

Lost time is never found again.

Who cannot obey, cannot command.
Conscience is the best policy.
Where there is a will, there is a way.
A home without a library is a home without soul.
All a woman asks is to be loved.
A woman can say more in a look than a man in a book.
Every man is the architect of his own fortune.

TEXT COMPREHENSION

1 Answer the questions:

a) Does forced love last for a long time?
___

b) Is it important to begin well?
___

c) Who cannot command?
___

d) Which is the best policy?
___

e) Which is the proverb that exalts the importance of books?
___

2 Match the columns:

A woman can say more in a look than •	• there is a way.
Where there is a will •	• to be loved.
All a woman asks is •	• out of mind.
Out of sight •	• a man in a book.
Two heads are better •	• blind.
All is well •	• the best policy.
Conscience is •	• than one.
Love is •	• when ends well.

LEARN THIS

Adverbs

Advérbios são palavras que modificam um verbo, um adjetivo ou outro advérbio.

She reads well. (Ela lê bem.)   **You are very intelligent.** (Você é muito inteligente.)
I live here. (Eu moro aqui.)   **She is very well.** (Ele está muito bem.)

Types of adverbs

1. **Time** (tempo):

Early	He came back early. (Ele voltou cedo.)
This morning	She arrived this morning. (Ela chegou esta manhã.)
Today	It is hot today. (Está quente hoje.)
Yesterday	I saw Mary yesterday. (Eu vi Mary ontem.)

Tomorrow	I will meet you tomorrow. (Eu me encontrarei com você amanhã.)
Tonight	I will stay home tonight. (Eu ficarei em casa esta noite.)
Next week	We will travel next week. (Nós viajaremos na próxima semana.)
Last month	I saw him last month. (Eu o vi no mês passado.)
On Saturday	They will arrive on Saturday. (Eles chegarão no sábado.)
In May	I was born in May. (Eu nasci em maio.)
At 7 o'clock	I get up at seven o'clock. (Eu me levanto às 7 horas.)
A week ago	He came here a week ago. (Ele veio aqui uma semana atrás.)

2. **Frequency** (frequência):

Frequently	I frequently go to the movies. (Eu vou frequentemente ao cinema.)
Never	My father never goes to the movies. (Meu pai nunca vai ao cinema.)
Rarely	I rarely make mistakes. (Eu raramente cometo erros.)
Seldom	I seldom go to the movies. (Raramente vou ao cinema.)
Sometimes	I sometimes visit my relatives. (Eu algumas vezes visito meus parentes.)
Often	I often see my girlfriend. (Eu frequentemente vejo minha namorada.)
Always	I always get up early. (Eu sempre me levanto cedo.)
Ever	Have you ever been to the U.S.? (Você já esteve nos Estados Unidos?)

3. **Manner** (modo):

Os advérbios de modo derivam de adjetivos e geralmente terminam com sufixo **ly**. Observe:

Rapid: rapidly	I rapidly understood the lesson. (Eu rapidamente entendi a lição.)
Polite: politely	She acts politely. (Ela age educadamente.)
Slowly	He reads slowly. (Ele lê vagarosamente.)
Carefully	She drives carefully. (Ela dirige cuidadosamente.)
Fluently	He speaks English fluently. (Ela fala Inglês fluentemente.)
Quickly	They went out quickly. (Eles saíram rapidamente.)
Patiently	We waited patiently. (Nós esperamos pacientemente.)
Hardly	I hardly go to the movies. (Eu dificilmente vou ao cinema.)
Badly	You read badly. (Você lê mal.)
Fast	She drives fast. (Ela dirige rápido.)
Well	She teaches well. (Ela ensina bem.)

Observações

Fast e well são exceções e não aceitam o sufixo **ly**.

4. **Place** (lugar):

Here	I live here. (Eu moro aqui.)
There	The ball is there. (A bola está lá.)
Upstairs	There are two bedrooms upstairs. (Há dois quartos no andar de cima.)
Downstairs	Come downstairs. (Venha para baixo.)
On the right	On the right there is a bank. (À direita há um banco.)
On the left	The church is on the left. (A igreja está à esquerda.)

5. **Intensity** (intensidade):
   Very   **She is very beautiful**. (Ela é muito bonita.)
   More   **She is more intelligent than John.** (Ela é mais inteligente do que John.)
6. **Negation** (negação):
   Not   **She is not well**. (Ela não está bem.)
7. **Affirmation** (afirmação):
   Yes   **Yes, he is late**. (Sim, ele está atrasado.)

ACTIVITIES

1 Form adverbs of manner by adding ly to the adjectives:

   a) clear   clearly

   b) sad _____   e) elegant _____   h) angry _____

   c) quick _____ f) brilliant _____ i) serious _____

   d) careful _____ g) anxious _____   j) violent _____

2 Complete the sentences with adverbs derived from the adjectives in parentheses:

   a) The teacher dresses. (elegant)   The teacher dresses elegantly.

   b) We waited for you. (anxious) _____

   c) We listened to the teacher. (attentive) _____

   d) I read the letter. (eager) _____

   e) We arrived. (punctual) _____

   f) She drives. (careful) _____

   g) She speaks. (polite) _____

   h) We walk. (slow) _____

3 Put the frequency adverb before the main verb and after the verb to be:

   a) I get up early. (sometimes)   d) I come to class on time. (always)

   I sometimes get up early.

   b) She was late. (never)   e) We go to the beach. (occasionally)

   c) The teacher speaks in a loud voice. (usually)   f) I visit my friends. (often)

4 Change the frequency adverb to English and insert it in the sentence:

a) **(frequentemente) I speak English.**
I frequently speak English.

b) (usualmente) I read the newspaper in the morning.
_____

c) (raramente) She goes to bed late.
_____

d) (nunca) I get up before 6.
_____

e) (sempre) I pay attention to class.
_____

5 Follow the pattern:

a) **Do you go to class in the morning? (in the afternoon.)**
No, I don't go to class in the morning. I go to class in the afternoon.

b) Do you get up at 6? (at 7)
_____

c) Do you have English classes on Fridays? (on Mondays)
_____

d) Did you go to the movies last week? (last month)
_____

e) Did you go to the movies yesterday? (the day before yesterday)
_____

LET'S SING

A time for everything

There is a time for everything:
A time to be born, a time to die.
A time to plant, a time to reap.
A time to laugh, a time to weep.
A time of war, a time of peace.
A time to work, a time to dream.
A time to hate, a time to love.
And a time for us, for you and me.

    Antes de cantar a música, ouça o professor ou o CD, prestando atenção na pronúncia das palavras. Procure, também, saber o significado delas.

Word bank

everything: tudo, cada coisa
laugh: rir
to be born: nascer
weep: chorar
die: morrer
dream: sonhar
reap: colher (verbo)
hate: odiar

Lesson 15

RELATIVE PRONOUNS

Thanksgiving Day (Dia de Ação de Graças)

Thanksgiving is a time to remember the Pilgrims, a group of settlers who came from England to start a new life in the United States.

They landed on the coast of the state of Massachusetts. They travelled from England on a ship named *Mayflower*, it took sixty-six days to arrive in the United States.

The Indians who lived nearby the coast showed the Pilgrims how to grow crops.

When the crops were ready the Pilgrims thanked God and the Indians. The Pilgrims invited the Indians to a feast in which they had a special dinner.

In the meal the Pilgrims thanked God for their food, their new friends and their new house.

It was the first Thanksgiving Day.

Today, Americans celebrate Thanksgiving on the fourth Thursday of November.

Americans celebrate the Thanksgiving on the fourth Thursday of November; Canadians on the second Monday of October.

TEXT COMPREHENSION

1. Who were the Pilgrims?
   _____

2. Where did the Pilgrims come from?
   _____

3. What was the name of the ship on which the Pilgrims came to America?
   _____

4. In which American state did the Pilgrims land on?
   _____

5. How many days did the Pilgrims' trip take?
   _____

6. Who lived nearby the Atlantic coast when the Pilgrims landed on America?
   _____

7. Were the Indians friendly to the Pilgrims?
   _____

8. Who helped the Pilgrims to grow crops?
   _____

9. What did the Pilgrims do when the crops were ready?
   _____
   _____

10. On the first Thanksgiving Day, whom did the Pilgrims thank?
    _____
    _____

11. The Americans celebrate Thanksgiving:
    ( ) in October
    ( ) in November
    ( ) in December
    ( ) on the third Thursday of December
    ( ) on the fourth Thursday of November

LEARN THIS

RELATIVE PRONOUNS

Who: que, quem (refere-se a pessoas); refere-se ao sujeito da sentença – é pronome sujeito. Observe:

The Indians who lived near the coast helped the Pilgrims.
(Os índios que moravam perto da costa ajudaram os peregrinos.)

Whom: a quem, de quem, para quem; refere-se ao objeto da sentença. – é pronome objeto (refere-se a pessoas). Veja:

That is the girl whom I invited to the party.
(Aquela é a garota a quem convidei para a festa.)

Whose: cujo, cuja, cujos, cujas.

That is the man whose son is my friend.
(Aquele é o homem cujo filho é meu amigo.)

That is the man whose farm I visited.
(Aquele é o homem cuja fazenda eu visitei.)

That: que (refere-se a pessoas, animais e coisas)

There are many birds that sing.
(Há muitos pássaros que cantam.)

The man that you saw is my father.
(O homem que você viu é meu pai.)

Which: que

The tomatoes which you chose are ripe.
(Os tomates que você escolheu estão maduros.)

Resumo

- Pronomes relativos que se referem a pessoas:
  who   whom   whose
- Os pronomes relativos **that** e **which** podem se referir a coisas, pessoas e animais.
- O pronome **that** pode substituir o pronome **who** e **which**.

ACTIVITIES

1 Follow the pattern:

a) **The man is my friend. He repaired my radio.**
The man who repaired my radio is my friend.

b) That is the girl. She telephoned me yesterday.

c) The man was following us. He was a policeman.

_____

d) The player scored that goal. He was Ronald.

_____

2 Join the two sentences by means of the relative pronoun that:

> **Observação**
>
> O pronome relativo **that** pode ter como antecedente uma pessoa, uma coisa ou um animal. Pode funcionar como sujeito ou objeto.

a) **He is the man. He helped me.** **He is the man that helped me.**

b) There is a girl on the telephone. She wants to speak to you.

_____

c) The story is very interesting. I read it yesterday.

_____

d) I know the man. He sent you a present.

_____

> **Observação**
>
> O pronome relativo **which** refere-se a coisas e animais e pode substituir o pronome **that**.

3 Join the two sentences by means of the relative pronoun which:

a) **That is the bird. It sings very well.** That is the bird which sings very well.

b) I like the picture. It is the living room. _____

c) I bought the car. It belonged to my grandfather. _____

d) She lent me a book. It was very interesting. _____

> **Observação**
>
> O pronome relativo **whom** tem como antecedente uma pessoa. Funciona como objeto e pode vir precedido de preposição.

4 Join the two sentences by means of the relative pronoun whom:

a) **You saw a man in the house. He was a thief.**

   The man whom you saw in the house was a thief.

b) The girl is my friend. You spoke to.

_____

c) The boy is my son. You telephoned yesterday.

_____

d) The girl is Mary. I love.

_____

e) This is the girl. I saw yesterday.

_____

f) The woman is my teacher. You saw last week.

_____

Observação

O pronome relativo **whose** tem como antecedente uma pessoa e significa: cujo, cujos, cuja, cujas; do qual, da qual, de quem, dos quais, das quais.

This is the man whose car was stolen. (Este é o homem cujo carro foi roubado.)

5 Join the two sentences by means of the relative whose:

a) **I know the man. His wife is a teacher.**   I know the man whose wife is a teacher.

b) That is the boy. His father is sick.   _____

c) This is the singer. I love his voice.   _____

d) He is the man. I admire his character.   _____

e) That is the woman. Her car was stolen.   _____

REVIEW

1 Choose the correct alternative:

a) I didn't see ***.
  ( ) something   ( ) anything

b) I know *** that you don´t know.
  ( ) anything   ( ) something

c) I have *** friends.
  ( ) much   ( ) few

d) There are *** flowers in the garden.
  ( ) several   ( ) little

e) There was *** in the room.
  ( ) somebody   ( ) anybody

2 Fill in the blanks using a relative pronoun:

Observação

Às vezes é possível optarmos por mais de um pronome relativo.

a) **The man who (that) repaired my radio is my friend.**

b) The man _____ is coming is the director of the company.

ninety-three 93

c) The player _____ scored that goal was Ronaldinho.

d) The policeman _____ was following us was Mr, Benson.

e) The story _____ I read yesterday was very interesting.

f) I like the picture _____ is in the living room.

3 Give affirmative and negative answers:

a) **Do you have any sugar?**

   Yes, I have some.

   No, I don't have any.

b) Do you have any money?

c) Do you have any games?

d) Do you have any work to do?

4 Change to the negative form:

a) **I saw somebody in the house.**   **I didn't see anybody in the house.**

b) There is some milk in the glass.

c) There is something to eat.

d) There are some boys in the class.

5 Change to the interrogative form:

a) **There are some birds in the tree.**   **Are there any birds in the tree?**

b) There is somebody in the car.

c) There are some books on the table.

d) She received a letter yesterday.

e) They found something in the house.

f) There are some letters for you.

FUN TIME

1 Opposites

What are the opposites of the adjectives below?

New → O ☐ ☐
Bad → G ☐ ☐ ☐
Cold → H ☐ ☐
Thin → F ☐ ☐
Poor → R ☐ ☐ ☐
Ugly → P ☐ ☐ ☐ ☐ ☐
Short → L ☐ ☐ ☐
Clean → D ☐ ☐ ☐ ☐
Difficult → E ☐ ☐ ☐

All dogs like bones!

Lesson 16

Also/too/either/neither

I live on a farm

Mike: Where do you live, Julie?
Julie: I live on a farm.
Mike: Do you like to live on a farm?
Julie: No, I don't.
Mike: Why?
Julie: Because I don't have any friends there and the nearest school is ten kilometers from my house.
Mike: Does your brother like to live on a farm?
Julie: No, he doesn't like it either.
Mike: And how about your father?
Julie: Oh, my father likes the farm very much. He hates the city.
Mike: And your mother, does she like the farm, too?
Julie: Yes, she also likes to live on the farm.

TEXT COMPREHENSION

1 Where does Julie live?
___

2 Does she like to live on a farm?
___

3 Julie doesn't like to live on a farm. Why?
___

4 How far is the school from Julie's house?
___

5 Do Julie's parents like to live on the farm?
___

LEARN THIS

ALSO – TOO – EITHER – NEITHER

Also: geralmente precede o verbo principal e, com o verbo **to be**, vem depois do verbo.
She also likes to live on a farm. (Ela também gosta de morar (viver) numa fazenda.)
We are also farmers. (Nós também somos fazendeiros.)

Too: geralmente aparece em final de frase.
Do you like to live on a farm, too? (Você também gosta de morar numa fazenda?)

Either: é usado na forma negativa.
I don't like to live on a farm either. (Eu também não gosto de viver numa fazenda.)

Neither: é usado em resposta a frases negativas.
– **I don't like to live on a farm**. (– Eu não gosto de morar numa fazenda.)
– **Neither do I**. (– Nem eu.)

Too: a palavra **too** significa demais quando precede um adjetivo ou advérbio.
The school is too far. (A escola está longe demais.)
The school is too dirty. (A escola está suja demais.)

ACTIVITIES

1 Insert **also**, **too** or **either**:

a) She doesn't like fish _____.

b) I go to the party _____.

c) She is _____ my daughter.

d) My teacher _____ likes Nature very much.

e) She is _____ rich and beautiful.

f) They like Brazilian music _____.

g) I don't understand German _____.

h) We love Nature _____.

i) They aren't in the class _____.

j) We don't watch television _____.

2 Use the word too before the adjective or adverb and translate the sentence:

a) **It is hot today.**
   It is too hot today. (Está quente demais hoje.)

b) **I can't buy the car. It is expensive.**
   I can't buy the car. It is too expensive. (Eu não posso comprar o carro. É caro demais.)

c) Yesterday I got up late.
   _____

d) It is early.
   _____

e) Very young girls can't wear much make-up.
   _____

f) I must eat something. I am hungry.
   _____

g) This lesson is difficult.
   _____

h) I am tired.
   _____

3 Follow the pattern:

a) I like milk. (I)   So do I. I like milk, too.

b) Mary sleeps early. (Helen)   So does Helen. Helen sleeps early, too.

c) I like coffee. (I)

d) Monica drives well. (Samia)

e) I work hard. (I)

f) John loves Andrea. (Jim)

g) Mary reads a lot. (Lucy)

h) Leny likes TV. (Doris)

i) Helen goes to bed late. (I)

j) Richard speaks English. (I)

4 Follow the pattern:

a) I don't like football.
Neither do I. I don't like football either.

b) I don't play tennis.

c) I don't drink coffee.

d) I don't speak English.

e) I don't understand Mandarin.

f) John doesn't have a motorcycle. (Paul)
Neither does Paul. Paul doesn't have a motorcycle either.

g) Betty doesn't go to the movies. (Jane)

h) Bob doesn't read the newspaper. (Tom)

i) Lucy doesn't like fish. (Richard)

j) My father doesn't sleep well. (my mother)

Lesson 17
GERUND AFTER PREPOSITIONS AND SOME VERBS

I like hot water!

Avoid wasting water, James!

Don't waste water!

James came home sweaty after a football match.

He was smelling unpleasantly, so he entered his bathroom and turned on the faucet of the bathtub to take a delicious bath.

His mother heard the water running and running for a long time.

– Why are you wasting so much water, James?
Turn off the faucet!

– Mom, I enjoy taking bath with plenty of hot water and this water is still warm...

– Avoid wasting water, James! Turn off the faucet!

– Ok, mom. I'll turn off the faucet when the bathtub is full.

– James, water is a limited resource of nature.
Be careful when you use it. You know, everybody needs water.

We can't live without water. It's up to everybody to use water wisely.

TEXT COMPREHENSION

1 How was James when he came back home after the football match?
_____

2 Why was James smelling unpleasantly?
_____

3 James turned on the faucet
( ) to take a shower   ( ) to take a bath in the bathtub

4 Why did James' mother reprehend him?
_____

5 James' mother asks him:
( ) to turn on the faucet   ( ) to turn off the faucet

6 James likes to take his bath:
( ) with cold water   ( ) with warm water   ( ) with hot water

7 Water is
( ) a limited resource of nature   ( ) an unlimited resource of nature

8 Can we live without water?
_____

9 Write the sentences under the appropriate pictures:

James is taking a bath in the bathtub.   James is taking a shower.

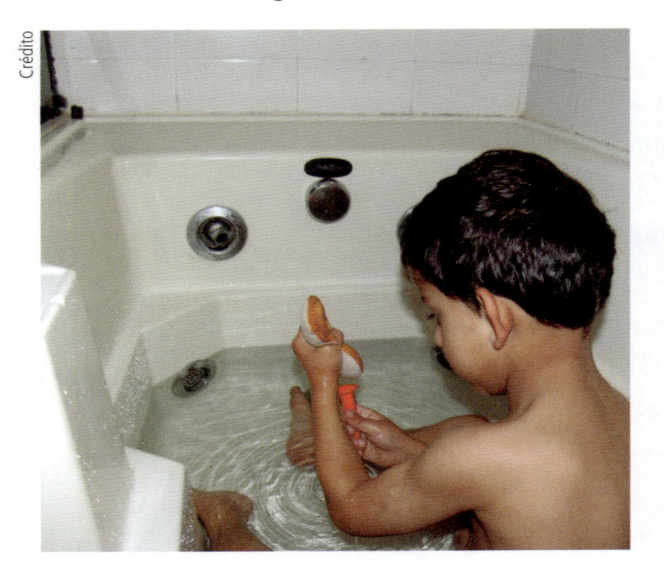

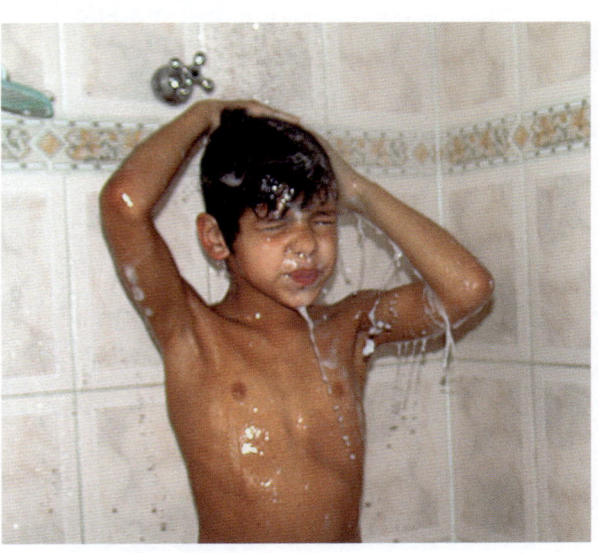

_____   _____

LEARN THIS

GERUND

1. **Gerund after some verbs → Gerund = verb + ing**
   Certos verbos exigem o gerúndio depois deles:

   enjoy (apreciar, gostar)
       I enjoy dancing. (Eu gosto de dançar.)

   avoid (evitar)
       I avoid wasting water. (Eu evito desperdiçar água.)

   stop (parar)
       We stopped studying. (Nós paramos de estudar.)

2. **Gerund or infinitive**
   Certos verbos permitem o uso do gerúndio ou do infinitivo:

   hate (detestar, odiar)
       I hate to get up early.
       I hate getting up early.
       (Eu detesto levantar cedo.)

   prefer (preferir)
       I prefer to stay at home.
       I prefer staying at home.
       (Eu prefiro ficar em casa.)

   like (gostar, adorar)
       I like to tell jokes.
       I like telling jokes.
       (Eu gosto de contar piadas.)

   forget (esquecer)
       I forgot to do my homework.
       I forgot doing my homework.
       (Eu esqueci de fazer meu trabalho de casa.)

   intend (pretender)
       They intend to study English.
       They intend studying English.
       (Eles pretendem estudar inglês.)

3. **Gerund after prepositions**
   Algumas palavras que regem preposições exigem o gerúndio:

   interested in (interessado em)
       I am interested in buying your car.
       (Eu estou interessado em comprar seu carro.)

   tired of (cansado de)
       I am tired of working. (Eu estou cansado de trabalhar.)

   ashamed of (envergonhado de)
       I am ashamed of making so many mistakes.
       (Eu estou envergonhado de cometer tantos erros.)

   give up (parar)
       I gave up smoking. (Eu parei de fumar.)

   difficulty in (dificuldade em)
       I have some difficulty in learning English.
       (Eu tenho alguma dificuldade em aprender inglês.)

ACTIVITIES

1 Answer affirmatively. Follow the pattern: verb + gerund

a) **Do you enjoy dancing?**   **Yes, I enjoy dancing.**

b) Do you like going out on weekends?
_____

c) Do you remember buying the medicine?
_____

d) Do you avoid speaking to strange people?
_____

e) Do you like traveling on your holidays?
_____

f) Did you finish writing the letter?
_____

2 Answer questions. Follow the pattern: verb + gerund

a) **What do you dislike? (get up early)**   **I dislike getting up early.**

b) What can't John resist? (eat sweets)
_____

c) What does Mary hate? (make her bed)
_____

d) What does the maid deny? (steal the watch)
_____

e) What does Mary admit? (go out with Bob)
_____

f) What do you remember? (take the keys from the drawer)
_____

g) What can't you tolerate? (the students arrive late)
_____

3 Use the gerund after the prepositions: preposition + gerund

a) **I have no intention of (leave) my country.**
   I have no intention of leaving my country.

b) I am fond of (dance).
_____

one hundred and three **103**

c) I have no difficulty in (find) the way.

d) He insisted on (go out) with us.

e) I need more practice in (drive) cars.

f) I have no experience in (sell) books.

g) I am tired of (walk).

4 Use the infinitive and the gerund. Follow the pattern:

a) I hate / eat fish   **I hate to eat fish.**   **I hate eating fish.**

b) He prefers / drink coffee

c) I like / swim

d) He started / eat the pizza

FUN TIME

Little elephant: I want to carry a piece of wood, too!
Mother elephant: A little one!

What has eight legs and sings?

104 one hundred and four

Additional texts

It is nice to live in contact with nature.

Nature

Flowers and trees, lakes and meadows, open spaces and wild forests are disappearing fast.

The incredible increase in number of human beings on the Earth, the spread of great cities, the pollution of our surroundings – all these things are destroying what we took as permanent: nature.

Our rivers are thick with pollution and the atmosphere is dark and dirty.

TEXT COMPREHENSION

1 Name some elements of nature that are disappearing.
_____
_____
_____

2 What is causing the destruction of Nature?
_____
_____
_____

3 Are our rivers clean?
_____
_____
_____

Nature gives us everything. Why destroy it?

Nature is beautiful and a source of life.

Observing nature attentively, we note that every being depends on the others.

Nature gives everything to man. Why destroy it? It's necessary to love and protect nature so that it can be a source of life for ever.

The Earth doesn't belong to man; it's mankind that belongs to the Earth.

TEXT COMPREHENSION

1 Is nature beautiful?

_____

2 Complete: "Nature is a source of _____."

3 Are all beings independent?

_____

4 What does nature give to man?

_____

5 Does the Earth belong to man or is the man that belongs to the Earth?

_____

one hundred and seven 107

Games – sports

A game is an activity that you generally practice for fun.

There are two types of games: indoor and outdoor games.

Today games are organized with a definite number of players, a definite area and with very rigid rules.

Games are very important to develop the body and to keep the mind healthy.

When you take part in a competition, the important is not to win but to compete.

It's necessary to win with modesty and know how to lose a game.

Fanaticism is the enemy number one of all kinds of sports.

By means of games and sports we can develop sociability and make new friends.

Games are very important to develop the body and to keep the mind healthy.

TEXT COMPREHENSION

1. What is a game?

2. What are the two types of games?

3. Are games important?

4 Complete: "It is necessary to win with _____ and know how _____."

5 What is the enemy number one in all kinds of sports?
_____

6 Complete: "By means of games and sports we can _____
_____

Patience is a virtue

The teacher drew on the blackboard a picture of a man sitting on the bank of a river.

The teacher: – You see this man. He is fishing. He must be patient and wait for a long time. All fishermen must have patience.

And the teacher insisted on the importance of patience as a great virtue. Finally he asked his pupils:

The teacher: – Now, can you tell me what do we need most when we go fishing?

The class in chorus: – Worms!!!

Since early times man has fished for food and fun.

TEXT COMPREHENSION

1 Who drew a picture on the blackboard?
_____

2 What did the teacher draw on the blackboard?
_____

3 Where was the man sitting?
_____

4 What virtue must all fishermen have?
_____

one hundred and nine 109

5 Did the teacher insist on the importance of patience?

_____

6 What did the class answer when the teacher asked:

"What do we need most when we go fishing?"

_____

7 Did the class understand the importance of patience?

_____

Young people like kart racing.

Hobby is an activity we do for pleasure.

Hobbies

Do you know what a hobby is? A hobby is a special way to spend free time. A hobby is an activity that we do for pleasure.

There are many kinds of hobbies. You can collect coins, stamps, rocks, buttons, shells, dolls, etc. If you like to work with your hands, you can choose clay modeling, collage, flower arranging, Indian beadwork, woodworking, soap sculpture, painting, etc.

Many people prefer outdoor hobbies such as cycling, camping, fishing, sailing, kite-making, etc.

A hobby may be a source of pleasure and teach us many things. It may be also the beginning of a new profession (occupation).

HOBBIES

MAKING COLLECTIONS

Antique collecting	Record collecting
Button collecting	Rock and mineral collecting
Coin collecting	Shell collecting
Doll collecting	Stamp collecting
Leaf and flower collecting	

Arts and handicrafts

Clay modeling	Leaf printing
Drawing	Leathercraft
Embroidery	Painting
Finger painting	Soap sculpture
Flower arranging	Woodworking
Indian beadwork	

Raising plants and animals

Aquariums	Dogs
Birds as pets	Gardens and gardening
Cats	Terrariums

Outdoor hobbies

Cycling	
Bird watching	Kite-making and flying
Boating	Mountain climbing
Camping	Sailing
Fishing	

TEXT COMPREHENSION

1 What is a hobby?
_____

2 Complete: A hobby is an activity that _____

3 Are there many kinds of hobbies?
_____

4 What can we collect?
_____

5 If you like to work with your hands, what can you choose?
_____

6 Mention some outdoor hobbies.
_____

7 Mention some advantages of hobbies.
_____

8 Complete: A hobby may be the beginning of _____

Vacation

When the school year is over, you will have some weeks of pleasant vacation.

What will you do?
Stay at home?
Take a trip?
Go to a camp?
Go to the beach?

A happy vacation will certainly make you calm and prepared to face life with new energy.

If you stay at home – If you stay at home, find out the activities offered by your community.

Your community will certainly offer you several kinds of sports and recreation, such as tennis, basketball, volleyball, football, cinema, theater, reading in public libraries etc.

Travel – One of the best pleasures in life is to travel. And there are so many interesting places to visit inside and outside your country!

When you travel you meet different people, see different customs and different places; you appreciate different food and drink. Life is wonderful when you travel.

Camping – A very interesting way to spend your vacation is to go camping. Camping develops your sociability and puts you in contact with nature.

Thousands of people go camping every year especially during summertime.

TEXT COMPREHENSION

1 Mention the alternatives you will have when the school year is over.
_____

2 Mention some advantages of a happy vacation.
_____

3 What is one of the best pleasures in life?
_____

List of irregular verbs

Infinitive	Past tense	Past participle	Translation	Infinitive	Past tense	Past participle	Translation
to be	was, were	been	ser, estar	to mean	meant	meant	significar
to become	became	become	tornar-se	to meet	met	met	encontrar-se com
to begin	began	begun	começar	to pay	paid	paid	pagar
to blow	blew	blown	soprar	to put	put	put	pôr
to break	broke	broken	quebrar	to read	read	read	ler
to bring	brought	brought	trazer	to ride	rode	ridden	cavalgar, andar a cavalo
to build	built	built	construir				
to burst	burst	burst	arrebentar	to ring	rang	rung	tocar a campainha, som do telefone
to buy	bought	bought	comprar				
to cast	cast	cast	arremessar	to rise	rose	risen	erguer-se
to catch	caught	caught	pegar	to run	ran	run	correr
to choose	chose	chosen	escolher	to say	said	said	dizer
to come	came	come	vir	to see	saw	seen	ver
to cost	cost	cost	custar	to sell	sold	sold	vender
to cut	cut	cut	cortar	to send	sent	sent	enviar
to deal	dealt	dealt	negociar	to set	set	set	colocar, fixar
to dig	dug	dug	cavar	to shake	shook	shaken	sacudir
to do	did	done	fazer	to shine	shone	shone	brilhar
to draw	drew	drawn	desenhar	to shoot	shot	shot	atirar, disparar
to dream	dreamt	dreamt	sonhar	to show	showed	shown	mostrar
to drink	drank	drunk	beber	to shut	shut	shut	fechar
to drive	drove	driven	dirigir	to sing	sang	sung	cantar
to eat	ate	eaten	comer	to sink	sank	sunk	afundar
to fall	fell	fallen	cair	to sit	sat	sat	sentar
to feed	fed	fed	alimentar	to sleep	slept	slept	dormir
to feel	felt	felt	sentir	to slide	slid	slid	escorregar
to fight	fought	fought	lutar	to slit	slit	slit	fender, rachar
to find	found	found	encontrar	to smell	smelled	smelled	cheirar
to fly	flew	flown	voar	to speak	spoke	spoken	falar
to forget	forgot	forgotten	esquecer	to speed	sped	sped	apressar-se
to freeze	froze	frozen	gelar	to spend	spent	spent	gastar
to get	got	got, gotten	conseguir	to spoil	spoilt	spoilt	estragar
to give	gave	given	dar	to spread	spread	spread	espalhar
to go	went	gone	ir	to spring	sprang	sprung	saltar
to grow	grew	grown	crescer	to stand	stood	stood	ficar de pé
to hang	hung	hung	pendurar	to steal	stole	stolen	roubar
to have	had	had	ter	to strike	struck	struck	bater
to hear	heard	heard	ouvir	to swear	swore	sworn	jurar
to hide	hid	hidden	esconder	to sweep	swept	swept	varrer
to hit	hit	hit	bater	to swim	swam	swum	nadar
to hold	held	held	segurar	to swing	swung	swung	balançar
to hurt	hurt	hurt	machucar	to take	took	taken	tomar
to keep	kept	kept	guardar	to teach	taught	taught	ensinar
to know	knew	known	conhecer	to tell	told	told	contar, dizer
to lay	laid	laid	pôr, deitar	to think	thought	thought	pensar
to lead	led	led	guiar	to throw	threw	thrown	arremessar
to learn	learnt	learnt	aprender	to understand	understood	understood	entender
to leave	left	left	deixar, partir	to wake	woke	woken	acordar
to lend	lent	lent	emprestar	to wear	wore	worn	vestir, usar
to let	let	let	deixar	to wed	wed	wed	desposar
to lie	lay	lain	deitar-se, jazer	to wet	wet	wet	molhar
to light	lit	lit	iluminar, acender	to win	won	won	ganhar, vencer
to lose	lost	lost	perder	to wring	wrung	wrung	espremer, torcer
to make	made	made	fazer	to write	wrote	written	escrever

General vocabulary

A

about: sobre, aproximadamente

above: acima

according to: de acordo com

achieve: alcançar

actor: ator

actress: atriz

address: endereço

admire: admirar

advantage: vantagem

advise: avisar

afraid: com medo

after: depois

again: de novo, novamente

ago: antes, atrás

agree: concordar

aim: finalidade, objetivo

angel: anjo

airplane, plane: avião

alive: vivo (a)

all: tudo, todo(a), todos(as)

all right: tudo bem

almost: quase

alone: sozinho(a)

a lot: muito, muitos

already: já

also: também

always: sempre

among: entre (muitos)

amplify: aumentar, ampliar

ancient: antigo(a)

appropriate: apropriado(a)

and so on: e assim por diante

angry: bravo(a)

another: outro(a)

answer: responder, resposta

any: nenhum(a), algum(a)

anything: qualquer coisa, algo

appeared: apareceu

around: em volta, ao redor

arranging: arranjo, arranjando

arrive: chegar

as: como

as...as: tão...como

ask: pedir, perguntar

assistant: assistente

astonished: espantado(a), atônito(a)

at: em, no ,na

at home: em casa

attentively: atentamente

atrium: entrada

attract: atrair

avoid: evitar

away: embora

awoke: acordou

B

baby: bebê

back: atrás, parte de trás

bad: ruim, mau

baker: padeiro

bakery: padaria

bank: banco

barber: barbeiro

bargain: barganha

base: base, basear

basket: cesta

bath: banho

bathroom: banheiro

bathtub: banheira

be: ser, estar

beach: praia

bead: borbulhar, conta

bean: feijão

bear: urso

beautiful: bonito(a)

beauty: beleza

became: tornou-se, ficou

because: porque

bed: cama

bedroom: quarto de dormir

beer: cerveja

before: antes

begin: começar

beginning: começo, começando

behind: atrás

beings: seres

believe: acreditar

bell: campainha, sino

belong: pertencer

below: debaixo

beside: ao lado

best: melhor (superlativo)

best-preserved: mais bem preservado

better: melhor (comparativo)

bighorn: carneiro selvagem

bill: conta

bird: pássaro

bird watching: observação de pássaros

birthday: aniversário

biscuit: biscoito, bolacha

bite: morder, mordida

blackboard: quadro-negro; lousa

blind: cego

blouse: blusa

blue: azul

board: tábua, prancha

boat: barco

boating: passeio ou esporte de barco

body: corpo

boiling: fervendo

bold: negrito

booming: explosão, estourando

border: limite, borda, fronteira

born: nascido(a)

both: ambos(as)

bottle: garrafa

bought: comprou

bowl: tigela

box: caixa

boyfriend: namorado

Brazilian: brasileiro

bread: pão

break: quebrar

brick: tijolo

bridge: ponte

bright: brilhante, radiante

broken: quebrado(a)

buffalo: búfalo

build: construir

building: construção, edifício, prédio

bus: ônibus

bus station: estação de ônibus; ponto de ônibus

busy: ocupado(a), atarefado(a)

but: mas

butter: manteiga

butterfly: borboleta

button: botão

buy: comprar

by: por

by means of: por meio de

C

cabbage: repolho

cake: bolo

call: telefonar, chamar

called: chamado(a)

camping: acampamento

can: posso, pode...

candy: bala, doce

can't: não posso, não pode...

canvas: lona

capital letter: letra maiúscula

care: cuidado

careful: cuidadoso(a)

carefully: cuidadosamente

car racing: corrida de carro

carry: carregar

catch: pegar, agarrar

caught: pegou

cause: causar

celebrate: celebrar, comemorar

cell phone: telefone celular

cement: cimento

certainly: certamente

change: mudar

chat: conversar

chatting: conversando

cheap: barato

check: verificar

cheese: queijo

chess: jogo de xadrez

chicken: frango

child: criança

childhood: infância

children: crianças

Chinese: chinês(a)

choice: escolha

chose: escolhi, escolheu

choose: escolher

citizen: cidadão(ã)

classsmate: colega de classe

clay: barro

clean: limpar

clear: claro

clerk: balconista, atendente

climb: subir

clip: clipe, grampo

close: fechar, perto

clothes: roupas

clothing: vestimenta

coach: técnico(a), treinador(a)

coast: costa

coin: moeda

cold: frio

collect: colecionar

come: vir

come back: voltar

comfortable: confortável

compare: comparar

complain: queixar

command: comandar, mandar

congratulations: parabéns

conscience: consciência

cook: cozinhar, cozinheiro(a)

cotton: algodão

correct: correto, corrigir

cost: custo, custar

could: podia, pôde

country: país, campo

courageous: corajoso(a)

course: curso

cousin: primo, prima

cover: cobrir

cow: vaca

crop: colheita

cross: cruzar, cruz

cup: xícara, taça

cupboard: guarda-louças; armário de cozinha

customs: alfândega

cycling: ciclismo

D

dam: represa, açude

daughter: filha

daily: diário

dangerous: perigoso(a)

dark: escuro

day: dia

dead: morto(a)

dear: querido(a)

death: morte

debt: dívida, débito

declare: declarar

deliver: entregar

deluge: dilúvio

deny: negar

desert: deserto

dessert: sobremesa

designed: planejado

desk: carteira

desperately: desesperadamente

develop: desenvolver

device: aparelho; invenção; projeto

devil: diabo

die: morrer

difficult: difícil

difficulty: dificuldade

dinner: jantar

dirty: sujo

disappearing: desaparecendo

dish: travessa, prato

dentist's: consultório dentário

disease: doença

dislike: detestar

dismissed: demitido(a)

do: fazer

doctor's: consultório médico

doggone: ora bolas! maldito! (no texto é um trocadilho para dizer o cachorro sumiu, foi embora: *the dog gone way*)

doll: boneca

done: feito

donkey: burro

don't: não

dotter: pontilhado

double: dobrar, dobro, duplo

down: baixo

drank: bebeu

draw: desenhar

drawer: gaveta, desenhista

drawing: desenho

dress: vestir, vestido

dressed: vestido(a)

drew: desenhou

drill: exercício, treino

drink: beber

drive: dirigir

drug: droga, remédio

drunkard: bêbado(a)

dry: seco(a)

due to: por causa de

E

eager: ávido(a)

early: cedo

Earth: Terra (planeta)

easily: facilmente

easy: fácil

eat: comer

egg: ovo

eight: oito

either: também

embroidery: bordado, ornamento

emperor: imperador

empty: vazio(a)

end: fim

ending: final

enemy: inimigo(a)

enjoy: usufruir, apreciar

enmity: inimizade

enter: entrada

establish: estabelecer

ever: sempre, já

every: cada

everybody: todos

everything: tudo

everywhere: em toda parte

exalt: exaltar

exam: prova, exame

examination: exame

examine: examinar

exclaim: exclamar

excuse me: desculpe-me

expensive: caro(a)

explain: explicar

F

face: face, enfrentar

factory: fábrica

faithful: fiel

fall: cair, outono, cachoeira

fall in love with: enamorar-se

famous: famoso(a)

far: longe

farm: fazenda

fast: rápido(a)

fat: gordo

father: pai

fatter than: mais gordo do que

faucet, tap: torneira

feast: festa

fell dead: caiu morto

fell in love: enamorou-se

fell: sentir, sentir-se

fellow: colega, companheiro

fence: cerca, grade

few: poucos

field: campo

fight: lutar

find: encontrar

fine: bom, boa, ótimo(a)

finish: terminar

fireworks: fogos de artifício

firm: firma

first: primeiro(a)

firstly: primeiramente

fish: peixe

fisherman: pescador

fishing: pescaria, pescando

fix: consertar, fixar

flag: bandeira

flour: farinha

flower: flor

fly: voar, mosca

fold: dobrar

follow: seguir

following: seguindo

fond of: fã de

food: alimento, comida

for: para, por

forbidden: proibido(a)

forced: forçado(a)

forget: esquecer

fortune: sorte

fortune-teller: adivinho, cartomante

foul: sujo(a), fétido(a), proibido(a)

found: achou, achado

fought: lutou

free: livre

French: francês(a)

fresh: fresco(a)

friar: frei

Friday: sexta-feira

fridge: geladeira

friend: amigo(a)

friendly: amigável, afável, simpático(a)

from: de (origem), desde

full: cheio

full form: por extenso

funny: engraçado(a)

G

game: jogo

gang: turma, grupo

garden: jardim

gardener: jardineiro

gardening: jardinagem

generally: geralmente

German: alemão(ã)

get: conseguir, ganhar, comprar

get hurt: machucar

get up: levantar

girl: garota, moça

give: dar

glass: copo, vidro

go: ir

goat: cabra

God: Deus

goal: gol, objetivo

goalkeeper: goleiro(a)

good: bom, boa

good luck: boa sorte

goods: mercadoria, bens

go to bed: ir dormir

go out: sair, saia

grain: grão

great: grande, ótimo

greatest: o maior

greatly: grandemente

grow: crescer, cultivar

grow up: crescer

guide: guiar, guia

guitar: guitarra, violão

gulf: golfo

H

hair: cabelo

ham: presunto

hand: mão

handsome: bonito, simpático, elegante

happy: feliz

hard: duro

has, has got: ele/ela tem

have, have got: ter

head: cabeça

health: saúde

healthy: saudável

hear: escutar

heard: escutado

heavy: pesado

help: ajudar

her: dela, a, lhe

here: aqui

herself: ela mesma, a si mesma

hen: galinha

hidden: escondido

high: alto(a)

higher: mais alto

him: o, lhe

his: dele

hobby: passatempo

hold: segurar

holiday: férias

hook: anzol

horn: chifre, corneta, buzinar

horse: cavalo

hot: quente

hour: hora

house: casa

how: como

how about: que tal

how long: que comprimento, quanto tempo

how many: quantos

how much: quanto

hundred: cem

hunger: fome

hungry: faminto(a)

hunter: caçador(a)

hunting: caça

I

ice: gelo

ice cream: sorvete

if: se

ill-bread: mal-educado

I'm going: eu vou

Impolite: grosseiro(a), rude

improve: melhorar

I'm sorry: sinto muito, desculpe-me

in bold: em destaque

Indian: índio, indígena

indoor: dentro de casa, em área coberta

in front of: na frente de

inhabitant: habitante

inquiry: investigar

interesting: interessante

intervened: interveio

intend: pretender

into: para dentro

invade: invadir

invite: convidar

island: ilha

it: ela, ele, o, a, lhe

items: itens

its: seu, sua

it's up to you: depende de você

J

job: emprego

join: juntar, unir

juice: suco

jump: pular

just: apenas

K

keep: guardar, manter

key: chave, tecla

kick: chutar

kill: matar

kind: tipo, espécie, bondoso(a)

kindness: bondade

king: rei

kiss: beijar

kite: pipa, papagaio

kite-making: confecção de pipas

kitchen: cozinha

knew: conheceu

know: conhecer, saber

known: conhecido

L

lake: lago

land: terra, desembarcar

landing: pouso, aterrissagem

language: língua (idioma)

landscape: paisagem

large: espaçoso(a), grande

largest: o maior, o mais extenso

last: último, durar

late: tarde

later: mais tarde

law: lei

lawyer: advogado(a)

lazy: preguiçoso(a)

leaf: folha

learn: aprender

leathercraft: trabalho em couro

leave: deixar, partir, sair

left: esquerda, deixou

lend: emprestar

lent: emprestou

less: menos

let's: vamos

let's go: vamos (ir)

letter: carta, letra

lettuce: alface

library: biblioteca

lie: mentir, mentira

life: vida

lift: levantar

like: gostar, como

lime: cal, lima (fruta)

linen: linho

lips: lábios

listen to: ouvir, escutar

little: pequeno(a), pouco

little by little: pouco a pouco

lives: vidas

living room: sala de estar

load: fardo

located: localizado

look: olhar, olhe

look for: procurar

lord: senhor, amo

lose: perder

lost: perdido

lot – a lot: muito

love: amar, amor

low: baixo

luck: sorte

lunch: lanche, almoço

luxury: luxo

luxurious: luxuoso(a)

M

machine: máquina

made: feito, fabricado, fez

made it up: fizeram as pazes

magazine: revista

magnificent: magnífico(a)

maid: empregada

mail: correio, depositar no correio

main: principal

majority: maioria

make: fazer, fabricar

make it up: fazer as pazes

make-up: maquiagem

man: homem

manager: gerente

Mandarin: mandarim (língua falada na China)

mango: manga

mankind: humanidade

manner: modo, maneira

many: muitos

many times: muitas vezes

mark: nota

marriage: casamento

marry: casar

marvelous: maravilhoso(a)

masked: mascarado

match: partida

matter: matéria, assunto, problema

may: posso, pode

me: me, mim, para mim

meal: refeição

meaning: significado

means: recursos, meios

measure: medir

meat: carne

medicine: remédio

meet: encontrar, conhecer (pessoas)

melon: melão

men: homens

mention: mencionar

merchandise: mercadoria

Merry Christmas: Feliz Natal

message: mensagem

messenger: mensageiro

met: encontro, encontraram

midnight: meia-noite

milk: leite

milk-jug: jarra de leite

mind: espírito, mente, importar

mistake: erro

mom: mãe, mamãe

Monday: segunda-feira

month: mês

morning: manhã

more: mais

more than: mais do que

mortar: argamassa

most: mais, a maior parte

mountaineering: escalada de montanha

mouse: rato, camundongo

mother: mãe

mud: barro, lama

must: precisar

N

name: nomear, citar

near: perto

nearby: nos arredores

nearest: mais próximo

necessary: necessário

need: precisar, necessitar

neither...nor: nem...nem

nest: ninho

never: nunca

next: próximo

new: novo

new year: ano novo

news: notícia, novidade

night: noite

no: não, nenhum

nobody: ninguém

none: nenhum

no-one: ninguém

north: norte

nothing: nada

noun: nome, substantivo

nor: nem, também não

northeast: nordeste

now: agora

nowadays: hoje em dia

number: número

O

occupation: profissão, ocupação

occupy: ocupar

odd: estranho, diferente

of: de

offer: oferecer, oferta

office: escritório

officer: oficial

often: frequentemente

old: velho

on: no, na, sobre

only: somente, apenas

on time: dentro do horário

open: abrir, aberto

opposite: antônimo

or: ou

orange: laranja

order: ordem, encomendar, pedir

other: outro(a)

our: nosso(a)

out: fora

outdoor: fora de casa, lado de fora

outside: exterior

over: acima, por cima

own: próprio(a)

P

pack: pacote, empacotar

packet: pacote

pad: plataforma

painting: pintura

paper: papel, jornal

parachute: paraquedas

parents: pais

party: festa

pass: passar

passing by: passando por ali

past: passado

patient: paciente

pay: pagar

peace: paz

peak: pico, cume

peasant: camponês

pen: caneta

pencil: lápis

people: pessoas

peoples: povos

perhaps: talvez

Persian: persa

persuade: convencer, persuadir

pet: animal de estimação

picture: quadro, figura, pintura

piece: pedaço

pig: porco

pilgrim: peregrino, romeiro

pin: alfinete, broche, pino

pineapple: abacaxi

pistol: pistola

place: lugar

plain: planície

play: jogar, brincar, tocar instrumento musical, representar uma peça, encenar

player: jogador(a)

please: por favor

pleased to meet you: prazer em conhecê-lo(a)

pleasure: prazer

plenty: quantidade, muito

plumber: encanador

poison: veneno

pole: vara

polish: polir

polite: polido(a), educado(a)

politician: político

poor: pobre

populous: populoso(a)

post: correio, pôr no correio

postcard: cartão-postal

postman: carteiro

pound: libra

power: poder, força

powerful: poderoso(a)

power station: estação de força

practice: praticar

precious: precioso(a)

predict: predizer

prejudice: prejudicar; preconceito

prescribe: prescrever

pretty: bonito(a)

price: preço

priest: padre

prince: príncipe

princess: princesa

profession: profissão

progress: progresso

proper: próprio, particular

protect: proteger

pull: puxar

punish: punir, castigar

pupil: aluno(a)

purpose: propósito

purse: bolsa

put: pôr

Q

quart: medida de líquido

queen: rainha

question: pergunta

quick: rápido

quickly: rapidamente

R

rabbit: coelho

race: corrida

rain: chover, chuva

raise: criar

rapidly: rapidamente

reach: alcançar

read: ler

ready: pronto(a)

reason: razão, motivo

receive: receber

recent: recente

record: disco

redeemer: redentor

referee: juiz; árbitro

refrigerator: geladeira

refuse: recusar

relatives: parentes

remaining: restante

remember: lembrar

repair: consertar

replace: substituir

reprehend: repreender

respect: respeitar, respeito

responsible: responsável

resist: resistir

resource: recurso

rest: descansar, parar, repouso, folga, pausa

return: voltar

rice: arroz

rich: rico(a)

rigid: rígido(a)

right: certo, direito

right now: agora mesmo

ring: anel, aro

ring: tocar (som da campainha, do telefone)

river: rio

rock: rocha, tipo de música

role-play: encenação

room: sala, cômodo

round: redondo, ao redor de

run: correr

S

sad: triste

sailing: prática da navegação

sail ship: barco a vela

same: mesmo

sand: areia

sat by: sentou-se ao lado

satisfy: satisfazer

Saturday: sábado

sausage: salsicha, linguiça

save: salvar, economizar

say: dizer

scientist: cientista

scissors: tesoura

score: marcar ponto (esporte)

season: estação

second: segundo(a)

secret: segredo

security: segurança

see: ver

seldom: raramente

selfish: egoísta

sell: vender

seller: vendedor(a)

send: mandar

sent: mandou

servant: servo(a), empregado(a)

shame: vergonha

shape: forma, formato

sheep: ovelha

shelf: estante, prateleira

shell: concha

shine: brilhar, brilho

ship: navio

shirt: camisa

shoes: sapatos

shop: loja

short: curto, baixo

shout: gritar

show: mostrar, espetáculo

shower: banho de chuveiro

shut: fechar

sick: doente

sight: vista

since: desde

sing: cantar

singer: cantor

sink: afundar, pia

sit: sentar

sit down: sentar

sitting: sentado, sentando

skin: pele

skirt: saia

sleep: dormir

slow: vagaroso(a)

slowly: vagarosamente

sluggish: mole

small: pequeno(a)

smallest: o(a) menor

smell: cheirar

smoke: fumar, fumaça

snack bar: lanchonete

so: tão, por isso

soap: sabão

soap-opera: novela

soccer: futebol

society: sociedade

solve: resolver

so many: tantos

some: alguns, algum, alguma, algumas

somebody: alguém

sometimes: algumas vezes

something: algo, alguma coisa

son: filho

sort: tipo, espécie

sorry: triste, preocupado

soul: alma

source: fonte

soy bean: soja

spaceship: nave espacial

speak: falar

specially: especialmente

spell: soletrar

spend: gastar, passar

square: quadrado

squirrel: esquilo

stamp: selo

stand: ficar de pé

star: estrela

starfish: estrela-do-mar

start: começar

state: estado

stay: ficar

steal: roubar

still: até

stolen: roubado

stone: pedra

stood: ergueu-se, ficou de pé, ficava

stop: parar

story: história

south: sul

strange: estranho(a)

street: rua

stretch: se estende

strong: forte

studious: estudioso(a)

study: estudar

subject: matéria, assunto

such as: assim como

suffer: sofrer

sugar: açúcar

suitcase: mala

suite: suíte

summer: verão

sunday: domingo

sunset: pôr-do-sol

sure: certamente, claro

surface: superfície

sweet: doce

sweaty: suado

Swiss: suíço

sword: espada

T

table: mesa

take: pegar, tomar, levar

take away: levar embora

talk: conversar

tall: alto(a)

tame: domesticar, domesticado(a)

tea: chá

teach: ensinar

teaching: ensinamento

team: time

teen: jovem (adolescente)

tell: contar, dizer

terrarium: terrário

than: do que

thank: agradecer

Thanksgiving: Dia de Ação de Graças

that: aquele, aquilo, aqueles, que

them: os, as, lhes

then: então, depois

these: estes(as)

this: este(a), isto

those: aqueles(as)

their: deles, delas

there: lá

there are: há (pl.)

there is: há (sing.)

thick: cheio(a), coberto(a)

thief: ladrão

thin: magro(a), fino(a)

thing: coisa

think: pensar

third: terceiro(a)

thirsty: com sede, sedento(a)

thousand: mil, milhar

throat: garganta

through: por, pelo, pela

throw: jogar, lançar, arremessar

Thursday: quinta-feira

tile: telha

till: até

time: tempo

times: vezes

tired: cansado(a)

toast: torrada

today: hoje

to him: para ele

tomato: tomate

tomorrow: amanhã

ton: tonelada

tonight: esta noite

too: também, demais

took: pegou

too much: demais

top: topo

topaz: topázio

to them: para eles

tower: torre

toy: brinquedo

traffic lights: farol, semáforo

training: treino

traitor: traidor

tranquil: tranquilo

tranquility: tranquilidade

translate: traduzir

travel: viajar, viagem

treatment: tratamento

tribe: tribo

trip: viagem

trousers: calça

truck: caminhão

truth: verdade

try: tentar, experimentar

Tuesday: terça-feira

turkey: peru

turn: virar

turn off: desligar

turn on: ligar

twin: gêmeo(a)

U

ugly: feio(a)

unconscious: inconsciente

under: debaixo

understand: compreender

understanding: compreensão

unfortunately: infelizmente

unknown: desconhecido

unlimited: ilimitado

unpleasant: desagradável

unpleasantly: de um modo desagradável, desagradavelmente

up: para cima

up to: acima de

us: nos, nós

use: usar

usually: geralmente

V

vaccinate: vacinar

vegetable: legume

vertigo: vertigem

village: vila

very: muito

very well: muito bem

villain: vilão(ã), covarde

voice: voz

W

wage: salário

wait: esperar

waiter: garçom

waitress: garçonete

wake: acordar

walk: caminhar, andar

wall: parede, muro, muralha

wallet: carteira

want: querer

war: guerra

warm: quente

was: era, estava

was born: nasci, nasceu

wash: lavar

waste: desperdiçar, lixo

watch: assistir, relógio

water: água

waterfall: cachoeira, catarata

watermelon: melancia

way: caminho, modo

wear: vestir

weather: tempo (atmosférico)

Wednesday: quarta-feira

week: semana

weekend: fim de semana

weigh: pesar, peso

well: bem

welcome: receber, saudar; bem-vindo(a)

you are welcome: não há de que, ao dispor

well done: bem-feito

were: éramos, fomos, eram, estávamos, estavam

whale: baleia

what: qual, o que

what a shame!: que vergonha!

what time is it?: que horas são?

what's she like?: como ela é?

when: quando

where: onde

whether: se

which: qual, que

whitewashing: caiação

who: quem, que

whom: a quem

whose: de quem; cujo(a); do(a) qual; eles(as), quais

why: por que

why not: por que não?

wife: esposa

one hundred and thirty-five 135

wild: selvagem

will: vontade

win: vencer, ganhar

window: janela

wine: vinho

winter: inverno

wisdom: sabedoria

wisely: sabiamente

with: com

without: sem

with us: conosco

wolves: lobos

woman: mulher

won: venceu, vencido

wonder: maravilha

wonderful: maravilhoso(a)

wood: madeira

woodworking: trabalho em madeira

wool: lã

word: palavra

work: trabalho, trabalhar

workplace: local de trabalho

worker: trabalhador(a)

world: mundo

worm: minhoca

worse: pior

worried: preocupado

would you like...: você gostaria...

write: escrever

written: escrito

wrong: errado(a)

Y

year: ano

yes: sim

yesterday: ontem

yet: ainda

young: jovem